The Complete Guide to Investing in Index Funds —

How to Earn High Rates of Return Safely

By Craig Baird

THE COMPLETE GUIDE TO INVESTING IN INDEX FUNDS: HOW TO EARN HIGH RATES OF RETURN SAFELY

1405 SW 6th Ave. • Ocala, Florida 34471 • 800-814-1132 • 352-622-1875—Fax
Web site: www.atlantic-pub.com • E-mail: sales@atlantic-pub.com
SAN Number: 268-1250

ISBN-13: 978-1-60138-205-4 ISBN-10: 1-60138-205-7

Library of Congress Cataloging-in-Publication Data

Baird, Craig W., 1980-
The complete guide to investing in index funds : how to earn high rates of return safely / by Craig W. Baird.
p. cm.
Includes bibliographical references and indexes.
ISBN-13: 978-1-60138-205-4 (alk. paper)
ISBN-10: 1-60138-205-7 (alk. paper)
1. Index mutual funds. I. Title.
HG4530.B25 2009
332.63'27--dc22

2008031813

Printed in the United States

PROJECT MANAGER: Melissa Peterson • mpeterson@atlantic-pub.com
INTERIOR DESIGN: Nicole Deck • ndeck@atlantic-pub.com
BACK COVER DESIGN: Nicole Orr • norr@atlantic-pub.com
COVER DESIGN: Shannon Preston

Dedication

To Layla, for allowing me to follow a new path.

We recently lost our beloved pet "Bear," who was not only our best and dearest friend but also the "Vice President of Sunshine" here at Atlantic Publishing. He did not receive a salary but worked tirelessly 24 hours a day to please his parents. Bear was a rescue dog that turned around and showered myself, my wife, Sherri, his grandparents Jean, Bob, and Nancy, and every person and animal he met (maybe not rabbits) with friendship and love. He made a lot of people smile every day.

We wanted you to know that a portion of the profits of this book will be donated to The Humane Society of the United States. ***–Douglas & Sherri Brown***

The human-animal bond is as old as human history. We cherish our animal companions for their unconditional affection and acceptance. We feel a thrill when we glimpse wild creatures in their natural habitat or in our own backyard.

Unfortunately, the human-animal bond has at times been weakened. Humans have exploited some animal species to the point of extinction.

The Humane Society of the United States makes a difference in the lives of animals here at home and worldwide. The HSUS is dedicated to creating a world where our relationship with animals is guided by compassion. We seek a truly humane society in which animals are respected for their intrinsic value, and where the human-animal bond is strong.

Want to help animals? We have plenty of suggestions. Adopt a pet from a local shelter, join The Humane Society and be a part of our work to help companion animals and wildlife. You will be funding our educational, legislative, investigative and outreach projects in the U.S. and across the globe.

Or perhaps you'd like to make a memorial donation in honor of a pet, friend or relative? You can through our Kindred Spirits program. And if you'd like to contribute in a more structured way, our Planned Giving Office has suggestions about estate planning, annuities, and even gifts of stock that avoid capital gains taxes.

Maybe you have land that you would like to preserve as a lasting habitat for wildlife. Our Wildlife Land Trust can help you. Perhaps the land you want to share is a backyard—that's enough. Our Urban Wildlife Sanctuary Program will show you how to create a habitat for your wild neighbors.

So you see, it's easy to help animals. And The HSUS is here to help.

2100 L Street NW • Washington, DC 20037 • 202-452-1100

www.hsus.org

Table of Contents

Putting Together a Portfolio 209

Managing YourIndex Fund Investment 221

Foreword

Because I am an investment banker and a former market maker at the Chicago Board Options Exchange (CBOE) and Chicago Stock Exchange, friends and family inevitably ask me for the latest tip or some sort of silver bullet in making sound, long-term investment decisions, and as much as I would like to reveal surprising or profound thoughts on this, the fact is that it is as simple as having a basic understanding of the stock market. However, that takes time in our busy lives, and we often need a quick, easy-to-understand outline to get us started. Fortunately, author Craig Baird has some great advice and provides a comprehensive overview for one of the foundations in sound investment: index funds.

It never ceases to astonish me how much people are willing to risk in the market during a strong economy and how much people hesitate in a weak one. The stock market, especially for short-term investors, is often volatile, and many people are hesitant to invest and find it difficult to pull the trigger.

When the economy is good, those individuals not heavily invested in stocks are thought of as social outcasts. How could you possibly sit out and miss these huge returns that everyone else is realizing? Back in the 1990s, it seemed like you could pick stocks by throwing darts and see double-digit returns.

And when things change for the worse, as they sometimes do, those investors who kept the diverse, cautious portfolios become the new experts. They may have missed some large returns, but they also missed some large losses. Everyone seems to be more anxious over the downturns than the upswings.

In today's world of hedge funds, credit swaps, and private equity funds, how can anyone possibly make sense of the infinite number of investment opportunities? While *The Complete Guide to Investing in Index Funds – How to Earn High Rates of Return Safely* does not explain the most recent, get-rich-quick scheme or identify the "best-kept secret" about investing, it does help you plan for a financially secure future. When looking forward to the future, even as far as retirement, understanding and utilizing index funds is a necessity.

Preparing for the unpredictable future is always a daunting task, and trying to accommodate for your retirement is even more complex. But Baird wonderfully describes steps that can be taken today to ensure financial security tomorrow. As I always tell the clients I am advising, capital markets are a great way to raise funds or jumpstart a project, but these markets are becoming increasingly more complex. There is much to gain, but also much risk, so it is crucial to understand exactly what is happening. Being able to look at your investment strategy and defend every option you choose may be difficult at times, but it is the best way to prepare for the future.

While the economy has and will continually fluctuate between good and bad, your long-term investment objective does not need to. If you understand index funds and use that knowledge while making investment decisions, you will be on your way to a strong and financially secure future. This book and the ideas outlined within it could not be more timely or important for investors during any economic cycle.

Alvin Boutte, Jr.
Managing Director, Midwest Region
Grigsby & Associates

Alvin Boutte, Jr. is the managing director of the Midwest Region for Grigsby & Associates, the nation's oldest, 100-percent minority-owned, full-service investment banking firm. An expert in investment banking and municipal finance, Boutte's distinctive background provides comprehensive financial services for a diverse base of clients.

Boutte's early interest in finance began under his father's tutelage, Alvin Boutte, Sr., from whom he learned to build and manage one of the most prominent and largest African American-owned financial institutions in the United States – Independence Bank of Chicago and Drexel National Bank (Indecorp).

The sale of Indecorp in 1995 provided Boutte an opportunity to move to the brokerage firm of Oppenheimer & Co., where he quickly established himself in emerging market business development and equity arbitrage. During this time, Boutte also became a member of the Chicago Board Options Exchange, Chicago Mercantile Exchange and the Chicago Stock Exchange, where he specialized in arbitrage activities.

Boutte later became partner in a local boutique investment bank and eventually cofounded DuSable Partners, where he developed a business that underwrites municipal bonds and increased exposure within the local pension plan community.

In addition to his work at Grigsby & Associates, Boutte is a board appointee of Chicago Mayor Richard M. Daley for the Illinois Sports Facility Board, the group that owns and operates U.S. Cellular Field. He also serves on the board of directors for the Mercy Home for Boys and Girls. Boutte is a graduate of Bradley University, with post-graduate studies at the University of Chicago.

About Grigsby & Associates

Grigsby & Associates is the second-oldest investment banking firm based in California. Since the firm's establishment as a corporation by Calvin Grigsby in 1981, Grigsby & Associates has helped local governments to raise more than $400 billion in tax-exempt capital for basic infrastructure, utility, housing, education, transportation, redevelopment, and general funding needs. In addition, the firm has helped arrange $10 billion in public and private corporate offerings.

Preface

There is a common misconception among passive observers of the stock market that what we see now has always been the norm, and little has changed over time since the first stock market was created. This is far from the case. The stock market constantly evolves, as do the economics and finances that drive it.

Early in the last century, the stock market was driven by railroads, steel, and oil, but much has changed. Now, new items like technology and software have created a different landscape. A trend has emerged in the last quarter-century, however, that has taken the stock market by storm; it has transformed the way things are done on Wall Street and all other financial headquarters around the world.

This trend is index funds, and while they proved to be a simple concept, it has taken decades for them to become mainstream investments. Indexing has become a simple, clean, and cost-effective solution to anyone's investing strategies.

Many think the stock market involves a group of investors picking stocks and getting rich. In fact, stock picking is considered one of the worst ways to invest in the market. Because many individuals and would-be investors do not see themselves picking the right stocks, they choose not to research the ways that stocks can be bought. As a result, they lose out on what could be big earnings.

Index-fund investing makes things easier for investors. It opens up the doors for millions of people to find the financial solutions they are looking for by understanding that the goal is not to beat the market — which is nearly impossible — but to replicate it. This leaves investors with less stress and more return. Understanding this will change the way you think about investing forever, and it will set out an entirely new path before you.

There is an old adage that a monkey could pick stocks by throwing a dart at the paper and investing in what it lands on; sadly, this is true. Countless studies have been done that prove that stock, time, manager picking, and all the other gimmicks that pass through the doors of Wall Street do nothing but rob people of their money through the art of gambling.

Through these gimmicks, you are taking money and putting it in something you hope will pan out for you. It may work, and you could reap big rewards — or it may crash and burn and rob you of your hard-earned cash. Everyone thinks they have a system to win in Vegas and, similarly, a system to beat the market on Wall Street. Think of Wall Street as a big casino: Everyone who goes there goes to gamble with their own tricks and techniques, believing they can win.

The stock market is so efficient that everything that can be known about a stock price is factored into the stock price. This efficiency means you cannot beat the market or predict what the market will do next. There are millions of people who tried and came up empty-handed, losing everything they owned and faced with having to start over again. For the few that did succeed, it was luck more than skill.

Of course, there is *one* way to beat the stock market, and that is to know the insider information on stocks before that information is released. This is called insider trading, but it could land you in one of the nation's many prisons — just ask Martha Stewart.

You can sit in front of a computer trying to bend the stock market to your will, choosing the stocks you think will succeed, or you can realize the truth: It is nearly impossible to beat the stock market, so do not try. Instead, make the choice to bend to another way of thinking about investing and go with index funds, a system in which you do not beat the stock market but, instead, you only replicate it.

Since their inception in the early 1970s, index funds have taken a long time to gain ground and become a popular form of investing. Nevertheless, through hard work and perseverance by the individuals who felt they had a truly revolutionary idea, the idea finally caught on.

There are currently trillions of dollars invested in hundreds of index funds around the globe. The index fund has become incredibly diverse, for everything from the Dow Jones to commodities.

Clearly, it has not been an easy road. At the turn of the twentieth century, those who conceived the idea of the "random walk," the basic idea behind the index fund, were scorned and laughed at. Through the mid-part of the twentieth century, investors did not see the point of pursuing something that offered average returns when they could attempt to pick stocks that would make them millionaires. But it would be the index fund theorists who would have the last laugh; many of them would go on to win the Nobel Prize in economics for their theories.

You may think there is too much to learn about index funds and that you will be bogged down in technicalities and financial jargon that will be difficult to understand. This is a popular misconception; however, index funds are surprisingly easy to understand, and by using them you can turn yourself from a would-be investor to a seasoned one.

Investing in the stock market does not have to be dangerous or foolhardy; it can be something you do with low risk and high rewards. Through the concept of the index fund, this is possible, and millions of investors are beginning to realize it.

So quit gambling on the stock market and tossing darts at a board. Start looking at investing in something that will actually make you money — an index fund.

This is not another gimmick to get rich quick: The established market has resisted it, but the Nobel Laureates have endorsed it. Turn off the so-called finance guru on television, put away any book or magazine that tell you they can make you a millionaire through stock picking or any other gimmick, and take the road to index funds.

Section 1

INTRODUCTION

Index funds are not a strange concept that only financial gurus understand. As we will see in this section, index funds are actually a simple concept. Despite being theorized by Nobel Laureates, even laypeople can understand index funds.

It all stems from the foundation of the index fund idea. The market is too random for anyone to be able to predict how it is going to function. With all the information relating to a stock already reflected in the stock price, there is no way to get a head start on the stock by anticipating what is going to happen. The stock market is so efficient it is almost impossible to beat. If you cannot beat it, what can you do?

We will see in Chapter One that an index fund is based on the theory of reflecting markets, not beating them. It is a safer way to invest and not worry about losing everything. Concepts such as asset allocation, diversification, and benchmarking will be introduced, none of which are difficult to understand.

In Chapter Two, we will see how the theory behind the index fund came from a French gambler more than 400 years ago. Put the theory together with the ideas of a surprising number of University of Chicago Booth School of Business graduates, and the index fund eventually evolved to change the way the stock markets operated forever.

In Chapter Three, after understanding the concept of an index fund and the history behind it, you will learn about the advantages it has over other types of investment strategies. The chapter will outline why active investors, stock pickers, time pickers, and others are considered to be nothing but gamblers. Learning about the advantages of the index fund will form the foundation for the next section of the book.

So, let us begin with an easy question: What is an index fund?

BD 09372045 A
FEDERAL RESERVE NOTE
ONE HUNDRED DOLLARS
100

1

What Is an Index Fund?

"Change is the process by which the future invades our lives, and it is important to look at it closely, not merely from the grand perspectives of history, but also from the vantage point of the living, breathing individuals who experience it."

-Alvin Toffler, Future Shock

You have been watching CNN, reading *The Wall Street Journal,* and you think you are ready to take the plunge and try your hand at investing in the stock market. At first, it may seem overwhelming trying to figure out exactly how and where to invest. Initially, we will concentrate on the New York Stock Exchange rather than the hundreds of stock markets around the world.

The stock market concept dates back to the eleventh century in Cairo, when Muslim and Jewish merchants set up trade associations and had knowledge of credit and payment. Because men traded with debts, they were the first to be called brokers. In the late thirteenth century, Bruges commodity traders gathered at a place called Van der Beurse, where Venetian bankers began to trade in government securities.

The first real stock exchange came into being in 1602 when the Dutch East India Company issued the first shares of the Amsterdam Stock Exchange. The Dutch created short-selling, option-trading, debt-equity swaps, unit trusts, and other types of speculative instruments. Consequently, the most important stock market, the New York Stock Exchange, sprang up in a city founded by the Dutch. Stock markets are now present in nearly every country, with the largest markets found in the United States, Canada, China, India, the United Kingdom, Germany, France, and Japan.

Heraclitus, a Greek philosopher, once said, "The only constant is change," and the stock market is proof of that. Change can come suddenly, like the stock market crash of 1929, which forced economists to rethink their methods. Or it can come in slow procession with different steps and foundations being laid; index funds, as we will find out, evolved from the latter.

Even though countless academics and some Nobel Prize winners touted the benefits of the index fund, the establishment resisted it, instead preferring to continue with the poor and illogical practices of stock picking and active investing.

As we will see at the end of this chapter and in Chapter 3, active investing and stock picking are two of the worst ways to manage a portfolio. It will often result in an individual losing what they own because of one poor decision.

The stock market can create wealth one moment, then crash down the next. The market could be accurately called "the great equalizer" because no one, rich or the poor, is immune to its effects.

The Index Fund Revolution, as it is called in this book, was a slow revolution that took decades to accomplish. Yet, as with most change, the more the establishment resists it, the harder it will push through.

An Index Fund, You Say?

An index fund is a collective investment, frequently in the form of a mutual fund, that has the goal of replicating, not beating, the movements of an index for a specific financial market. Index funds have a set of rules for ownership that are held constant, regardless of the conditions of the stock market. Investors can track an index through the holdings of securities in the index in the same proportions as the index itself. There are several other methods to using an index fund, including holding representative securities and statistically sampling the market. More often than not, index funds rely on a computer model with little or no human input when deciding which securities are purchased. Index funds, as a result, are a form of passive management and, because there is no active management, fees and taxes are lower, leaving a higher return for the investor.

There is no way the index fund can mirror the index completely. The difference between the index fund performance and the index performance is known as the tracking error, which is usually low.

Many investment managers offer index funds: the Standard and Poor's 500, the Wilshire 5000, the FTSE 100, and the FTSE All-Share Index are just a few examples.

Index funds have become increasingly popular due to their method of replicating an index rather than beating it. When a fund is attached to a specific index, it is called benchmarking.

What Is Benchmarking?

Benchmarking is an index that serves as a standard against which the performance of the fund or portfolio is measured. Almost all investment portfolios are benchmarked to one or more indexes. An investor can gauge the performance of that portfolio by comparing the risks and return of a portfolio to an appropriate index or set of indexes.

For example, if a group of stocks increased 10 percent last year, one might assume it was an excellent year. However, without being able to measure it against a benchmark, you cannot know for sure. If the S&P 500 only gained 5 percent last year, then that group of stocks did an excellent job; conversely, if the S&P 500 gained 20 percent, the great year comparatively looked poor.

Benchmarking should be done on a quarterly basis; doing so more often will result in inconsistencies between the return of a market index and the cash flow return of a portfolio. These inconsistencies normally cancel each other out by the end of a quarter.

When looking at the difference in performance between an index fund and its benchmark, economists will look at the tracking error. The ideal index fund tracking error is 0 percent with the benchmark, but this is nearly impossible. Instead, a .25 percent per year tracking error is considered the best.

The Dow Jones Industrial Average

Before the turn of the twentieth century, the Dow Jones Industrial Average was created to give investors a way to view an index of stock prices. It initially covered only 12 stocks and gave people the ability to view the index as a measure of stock prices against the value of the index.

The first companies listed on the stock were:

1. American Cotton Oil Company
2. American Sugar Company
3. American Tobacco Company
4. Chicago Gas Company
5. Distilling & Cattle Feeding Company
6. Laclede Gas Light Company
7. National Lead Company
8. North American Company
9. Tennessee Coal
10. Iron and Railroad Company
11. U.S. Leather Company
12. U.S. Rubber Company

The first average of the Dow Jones was 40.94. The Dow Jones Industrial Average used just 12 stocks to get its average value, so computation was easy. Basic math skills could add up the values of the stocks for that day and divide by 12. Even though there were other stocks that could have been included, the Dow Jones Industrial Average and its 12 stocks became the leading index in the world, as it still is today. *The Wall Street Journal* (which Charles Dow, cofounder of Dow Jones and Company, owns) uses the Dow Jones as its leading index. The Dow Jones Industrial Average would eventually increase the number of stocks it indexed to 20 in 1916 and 30 in 1928, which is where the Dow Jones remains today.

The Dow Jones works by basing point movements of stocks rather than the percentage movements. This means a $1 gain on a $10 stock has the same impact on the Dow Jones as a $1 gain on a $100 stock. While the gain is the same, the percentage in terms of the stock price is not. This leads to a distortion between the index price and the market values, which is the biggest drawback of the Dow Jones Industrial Average.

Because the Dow Jones does not capture the value movements of companies, it is a poor index. The Dow Jones only captures the price movements, which do not fit well in attempting to measure the overall value of the stock market. Also, the Dow Jones only represents 30 stocks — a far cry from the current number of stocks on the market, which is roughly 5,000 stocks.

The Dow Jones is a limited and out-of-date measure of today's stock market as it cannot measure proper performance, direction, or level of the stocks listed on all the U.S. stock exchanges. While many realized this early on, it would take nearly 30 years before a more comprehensive index was created.

The S&P 500

In 1923, the first Standard and Poor's (S&P) index was introduced. It comprised 90 companies, became known as the S&P 90, and was published on a daily basis. In addition, a broader index of 423 companies was published weekly.

On March 4, 1957, the flagship of the company was introduced. Known as the S&P 500, it provides a broad, real-time stock market index to investors.

Without the aid of a computer, it would have been a monumental task to compile the average of 500 stocks on a daily basis. Nevertheless, technology caught up with the stock market and created a market-weighted index.

A market-weighted index means that if a large company's stock increases, it would have a greater effect on the market than if a smaller company's stock increases. For example, Ford Company's value is greater compared to the Pangaea Petroleum Corporation that trades under $5 and is considered a penny stock.

The S&P 500 is used widely now as an indicator of the broader market. It includes growth stocks, less volatile value stocks, and stocks from the NASDAQ and New York Stock Exchange. Growth stocks have the potential to rise quickly, giving big profits but coming at a high risk. An excellent example of growth stocks are those that inflated and deflated in the dot-com bubble. Value stocks are in a company that is a leader in its industry and has been an established company for many decades.

The S&P 500 reached its all-time intraday high of 1,552.87 in trading on March 24, 2000. It then lost 50 percent of its value in a two-year bear market, causing it to drop below 800 points in July 2002 and reach a low of 768.63 on October 10, 2002. On May 30, 2007, the S&P 500 closed at 1,530.23 to set its first all-time closing high since the bear market collapse in 2002.

Other Indexes

A wide variety of indexes exists, all of which range in size from the exceedingly large to the very small. Some were created by the pioneers of the index fund movement, while others are based on size, industry sector, or country. Also, indexes are not limited to U.S. markets: The Nikkei Stock Average, the most quoted index in Japan, has an average of 225 leading stocks that trade on the Tokyo Stock Exchange.

Bond Market Indexes

Markets that specialize in bonds, often called credit or fixed-income markets, also have indexes including the U.S. Treasury, corporate, high-yield, convertible, tax-exempt, and foreign bonds. These types of indexes differ from stock market indexes in terms of their complexity.

The Bond Market Index reflects the composite value of index components and is used as a tool to represent the characteristics of its component fixed income instruments. These types of indexes are often more complex than a stock index.

With these varied types of bonds, there is also a great deal of variety among bond indexes. One of the primary ways of distinguishing between bond indexes is the quality of the bond. High-yield bonds, or junk bonds, have a higher risk than Treasury bonds, but they also pay out at a higher interest rate.

We will briefly outline some of the more popular types of bonds.

Government Bonds

A government bond is issued by a national government in the government's own security. If a bond is released by the national government in a foreign currency, then it is referred to as a sovereign bond. These are also called risk-free bonds because the government can raise taxes or print more money to redeem the bond at maturity. However, there have been cases where the government defaulted on domestic currency debt, as Russia did in 1998 during the Ruble Crisis.

Corporate Bonds

A corporate bond, as the name implies, is a bond a corporation issues that normally applies to long-term debt instruments with a maturity date that falls at least a year after the issue year. Corporate bonds are often listed on the major exchanges of the world, and the interest payment of a corporate bond is often taxable. Most of the trading volume of corporate bonds in developed markets takes place in decentralized, dealer-based markets. Some corporate bonds have a call option that allows the issuer to redeem the debt before it hits its maturity date, while other bonds, called "convertible," allow investors to convert the bond into equity. There is a greater risk of default on corporate bonds when compared to government bonds, but this depends on the corporation, market conditions, and the rating of the company.

High-Yield Bonds

A high-yield bond is a bond rated below investment grade at the time it was purchased, resulting in a higher risk of default. However, the added risk of default comes with the benefit of higher yields when compared to other bonds.

Characteristically, most issuance is done in the United States, with some issuers in Europe, Asia, and South Africa turning to high-yield debt in connection with refinancing and acquisitions. The holder of debt on a high-yield bond is subject to interest rate risk (the risk of the market value of a bond changing in value due to changes in the structure of level of interest rates) and credit risk (the probability and probable loss upon a credit event).

Mortgage-Backed Securities

A mortgage-backed security is an asset-backed security that has cash flow and is backed by principal and interest payments from a set of mortgage loans. These payments are frequently paid over the lifetime of the loan(s) on a monthly basis.

Commercial mortgage-backed securities are secured by commercial and multi-family properties such as apartment buildings, retail properties, or office buildings. The properties on these loans are pre-payable vary from long-term loans at fixed interest rates to smaller loans with variable interest rates.

Passive Investment Management and Bond Indexes

Bond indexes are harder to replicate for an index fund than stock market indexes due in part to the average duration of the market, which may not be an appropriate duration for a portfolio.

Despite this, replication can be achieved by using bond futures to mature the duration of the bond index.

Bond Indexes

The following are several bond indexes that an investor can consider. We will outline them briefly to give an idea of where investors can go when they are interested in pursuing a portfolio that replicates a bond index.

Lehman Aggregate Bond Index

This is a broad-based index with index funds and exchange-traded funds available on it; it is used to represent investment grade bonds being traded in the United States. Managers will often subdivide parts of this index by maturity or sector to help in the management of portfolios. In August 2002, Barclays Bank created the iShares Lehman Aggregate Bond Exchange-Traded Fund to reflect the performance of this index.

Merrill Lynch Domestic Master

This is a common bond index that is analogous to the S&P 500 for stocks and rebalances on the last calendar day of every month. This index was created December 31, 1975, as part of the larger Merrill Lynch U.S. Broad Market. This index excludes asset-backed securities; tax-exempt municipal debt; 144As; any bond without a fixed coupon schedule or less than $1 billion outstanding for U.S. Treasuries; and $150 million for all other securities.

Merrill Lynch High Yield Master II

This bond index is commonly used as a benchmark for high-yield corporate bonds by providing a measure of the broad high-yield market, unlike the Merrill Lynch BB/B Index, which excludes lower-rated securities.

Stock Markets vs. Stock Indexes

With all this talk of stock indexes and stock markets, some people may become confused and think stock markets and stock indexes are the same; however, they are different concepts.

A stock market is when shares of stocks are traded between investors using stockbrokers as their agents. The New York Stock Exchange is the best example, as more than 2,700 stocks change ownership there. Another example is the NASDAQ, or National Association of Securities Dealers Automated Quote system, where stocks and bonds trade through cyberspace. The NASDAQ is a computerized market system that links brokers and dealers together, helping them trade stocks over the counter. This is often considered to be the best representation of new-economy stocks for technology companies.

A stock index is a measure of the value of a stock market. The S&P 500 is a stock index created by a market that measures the value of 500 stocks selected by the S&P Index Committee. These types of indexes are commonly considered secondary to indexes that cover all markets. For example, exchange-created indexes hold only those stocks that trade on a particular exchange. For instance, Microsoft and Google™ trade on the NASDAQ stock exchange, so they are not listed on the New York Stock Exchange Composite Index.

One of the most popular index funds on the NASDAQ is the NASDAQ 100 Tracking Stock, whose objective is to provide investment results that correspond to the price and yield performance of the largest 100 stocks on the NASDAQ.

The Usefulness of the Indexes

Stock markets and other indexes are considered useful because they allow economists to gauge the wealth of the nation based on the performance of particular indexes. They can also be used to track the consumers' moods, which, in turn, can help forecast sales, profits, and economic growth. Also, indexes can be compared to each other. By using the spread between them, economists can gain an understanding of investors' attitudes and foresee possible trading opportunities.

The most important use of the index is its role as a benchmark for mutual fund management. To create a benchmark, guidelines established by the Chartered Financial Analyst Institute must be met: relevance, comprehensiveness, replication, stability, barrier to entry, expenses, and simple and objective selection criteria.

Relevance

For an investor to be interested in an index, the index needs to be relevant to them. This means that the index should at least track the markets that are of the most interest to the investor.

Comprehensive

The core point of index funds is the broad range they cover in the stock market, often with a vast number of stocks in their portfolio. As a result, an index should have all the opportunities that are available to an investor under normal market conditions. At the same time, it must keep a measurement of the performance of any investments and holdings the investor may have.

Able to Replicate

If only one investor can achieve certain results with an index portfolio, there is little reason for other investors to take part and attempt to benefit; the returns on an index need to be replicable for all market investors. The index needs to be fair to investment managers and also to sponsors who pay fees or award management assignments. The index should also have a baseline strategy that can be followed by a passive investor over time. This means that information, including historical, should be available to investors regularly.

Stability

For an index to succeed, it needs to be relatively stable. If changes occur, they must be understood. Index composition must change often enough to ensure it reflects accuracy and structure in the market. The index must act as a benchmark for investors so they are not forced to keep pace with it by executing a large number of transactions.

No Barrier to Entry

If no one can take part in the index, then there is little point to having one. An index, especially international indexes, should not have any significant barriers to entry.

Expenses

Expenses regarding taxes and transactions will inevitably occur for an investor. For an index to succeed, these extra expenses must be easily understood by investors in the market and should not be too high. Therefore, expenses cannot be unpredictable for an index to measure market performance.

Simple and Objective Selection Criteria

Rules for an index need to be clear and govern the inclusion of bonds, equities, and markets in an index. This allows investors to attempt to forecast and reach a consensus on changes that will occur in composition.

What is a Mutual Fund?

On March 21, 1924, the Massachusetts Investors Trust was formed, and in one year it had 200 shareholders and $392,000 in assets. By 1924, the entire industry of mutual funds was worth around $10 million.

As with most financial matters, the stock market crash of 1929 slowed the growth of mutual funds. In response, Congress passed the Securities Act of 1933 and the Securities Exchange Act of 1934, which required a fund to register with the Securities and Exchange Commission (SEC), providing investors with a prospectus that contained disclosures about the fund, the securities, and the fund manager. The SEC then drafted the Investment Company Act of 1940, setting guidelines that all SEC registered funds must comply with.

Once the stock market began to recover, mutual funds took off, and by the end of the 1960s, there were 270 funds worth $48 billion in assets. One of the largest contributors to mutual fund growth was the individual retirement account (IRA) that allowed individuals to contribute $2,000 per year from their corporate pension to a mutual fund; these have now become as popular as 401(k)s.

As of October 2007, there were 8,015 mutual funds that belonged to the Investment Company Institute, which is the National Association of Investment Companies in the United States, with combined assets of $12.4 trillion.

Types of Mutual Funds

As a rule, most investment portfolios are benchmarked to one or more market indexes because an investor can compare the risk and return of a portfolio to an appropriate index or set of indexes and calculate the performance of the entire portfolio.

Mutual funds are preferred by many investors because they offer diversification, ease of management, and tax simplification at a low cost. For this reason, mutual funds are popular. One commonality between many types of mutual funds is the fact that the money manager has the right to buy or sell any type of mutual fund as he or she sees fit. Some mutual funds profiled here will be discussed in more detail in later chapters.

Open-End Mutual Funds

Open-end mutual funds use a large group of investors that pool their money into an account that is held in trust. A professional money manager is hired to pick shares with each investor, owning a certain number of shares based on the amount of money they put into the trust. If an investor chooses to sell their shares, they sell back to the trust at the end of the trading day when the fund manager sells stocks and bonds to raise the cash needed to pay the investors.

The biggest difference between open-end mutual funds, compared to closed-end and exchange-traded mutual funds, is that shares of closed-end and exchange-traded mutual funds are traded on the stock market during the day, rather than within the fund company at the end of the day, as open-end funds do.

Exchange-Traded Funds

Exchange-traded funds (ETFs) are formulated as an open-end investment company that combine characteristics of both mutual funds and closed-end funds, often tracking a stock index. With an exchange-traded fund, shares are issued by investors in large blocks, normally 50,000. Because investors handle the majority of the trades with ETFs, they are more efficient than traditional mutual funds, which create lower expenses.

Equity Funds

Equity funds comprise stock investments and are the most common type of mutual fund, holding 50 percent of all amounts invested in mutual funds in the United States. These funds focus investments on particular strategies and certain issuers.

Capitalization Funds

Fund managers and other professionals will often define a fund based on its market capitalization. There are four types of market capitalization mutual funds: Large-Cap, Mid-Cap, Small-Cap, and Micro-Cap. These will be profiled in more detail in Chapter 4.

Growth Funds

Growth funds appreciate in value and yield a high return on equity. The return on equity is taken by looking at the company's net income and dividing it by the company's equity. To be classified as a growth fund, a company must have at least 15 percent return on equity.

Value Funds

Value funds have had a history of good market performance from an established company that is a leader in its industry. These are frequently a safe investment that has low risk but also low yield.

Bond Funds

Bond funds currently account for 18 percent of all mutual fund assets, with types of funds including term funds that have a fixed term; municipal bonds that have low returns but lower risk; and junk bonds, also called high-yield bonds, that were discussed earlier.

Money Market Funds

These funds hold 26 percent of the mutual fund assets in the United States. They have the least amount of risk and a low amount of return; they are also liquid and can be redeemed at any point.

Funds of Funds

This variety of funds invest in other underlying mutual funds, which are normally funds that an investor can invest in individually. They charge a management fee that is smaller than a normal fund because it is considered a fee charged for asset allocation services. Most funds of funds invest in affiliated funds, which are managed by the same advisor.

They are structured to provide a ready mix of mutual funds for investors that are unable or unwilling to determine their own asset allocation model. Companies that offer this help to assist investors include Vanguard and Fidelity. The allocation mixes regularly vary by the time the investor would like to retire, whether it is 10, 20, or more years from now. The more distant the target retirement, the more aggressive the asset mix.

Why Have Mutual Funds?

There are three main reasons to own mutual funds. Most of us do not have the time or experience to look at each stock or bond to determine which is the best to buy. Also, most mutual fund managers are well-educated and have attended school to earn degrees in economics and finance.

Furthermore, about half of all mutual fund managers hold the Chartered Financial Analyst distinction. And an investor simply cannot look at all the stocks, read all the financial publications, and watch all the financial news shows to get the rundown on everything; there is too much information available for one person to constantly monitor.

Of course, with so many mutual funds out there, it can be hard to find the right one for you. This is where index funds come in.

Mutual Funds Beget Index Funds

An index fund is a type of mutual fund, with most index funds being open-ended. Though they fall under the mutual fund category, there is a difference that sets the index fund apart: An index fund manager does not have as much discretion regarding an investor's investment into a fund as a mutual fund manager would have.

Index funds also differ from active funds in that an active fund portfolio manager can use his or her own judgment to determine which stocks will go into the fund and which will come out. Index fund managers must follow the benchmark index composition as closely as possible, which means holding a share of each stock or bond in the index.

It is important to understand that index funds are not meant to beat a benchmark, like a mutual fund, but to mirror it.

Myths of Index Funds

Rumors surround the use of index funds, and most of them come from investors who have resisted changes in how the stock market operates, refusing to become part of the index fund revolution.

There is a prevalent myth that index funds work only in bull markets; this is far from the case. This myth came about because of the perception of active managers who tended to be more defensive during periods of market under performance, volatility, or non-trending market performance. Thus, they post better results than blind indexing strategies during those periods of bear markets.

Some believe that indexing's success will drive out successful active managers; however, investment money is still actively managed. Professional security analysts and other money managers are far from being driven out of the industry.

The Types of Indexing

There is typically more than one way to accomplish a task, and indexing is no different. Here are several methods that have been used over time by a variety of investors. These types are traditional, synthetic, enhanced, leveraged, and inverse.

Traditional Indexing

For indexing to be known as traditional, an investor must own a representative collection of securities that are in the same ratio as the target index. Any modifications to security holdings only occur when a company leaves or enters the target index. An example of a traditional index fund is Barclays iShare®, which trades on the Russell 2000 Value Index. This index frequently contains companies with lower price-to-book ratios and long-term growth. Another example of a traditional index fund is the Vanguard 500 index fund that has accumulated more than $70 billion in assets, despite being criticized when it was launched by the Vanguard Group in 1976.

Some experts in the field are beginning to feel that traditional indexing is flawed, including Bruce Bond, who started PowerShares in 2002. In an interview with **www.MarketWatch.com** on Nov. 27, 2006, Bond said, "The main problem is that the well-known benchmarks rank stocks according to market value, or capitalization. By default, the biggest stocks dominate the index regardless of their investment or business merit and expose investors to undue risk."

Synthetic Indexing

This is a modern technique that requires a combination of equity index futures contracts and investments in low-risk bonds. This indexing replicates the performance of a similar overall investment in stocks that comprise an index.

Synthetic indexing maintains a higher position in the future at a slightly higher cost structure than traditional indexing and can be favorable toward tax treatment, especially for international investors that are subject to U.S. tax laws.

This form of indexing does not invest directly in stocks; rather, by using derivatives, it enables an investor to realize the return of an index for a specified period of time. These funds are frequently developed and managed by index fund managers such as State Street Global Advisors, Barclays Global Investors, Northern Trust Global Investments, and Mellon Capital.

These provide investors with restrictions and actions that can be directly imposed on the holding of the assets. This can also alter the tax impact of an asset exposure because synthetic index funds are considered ordinary income, not capital gains.

Enhanced Indexing

This type of indexing is often deemed the "catch-all" when referring to improvements to index fund management. The type of management associated with enhanced indexing is one that emphasizes performance using active management.

These types of index funds use an array of techniques, including customized indexes, trading strategies, exclusion rules, and timing strategies. The overall cost of this form of indexing is often reduced or eliminated through active management. The underlining idea of enhanced indexing is to eliminate the risk of under performing a market by tracking the returns of that market.

Investors will often make minor changes to a good index in the effort to beat the benchmark of the market by even the smallest amount. If the investor fails because of these minor changes, there will be a relatively small tracking error against the benchmark.

There are two main types of index enhancement that we will cover.

SECURITY-BASED ENHANCEMENT

These enhancements start from an assumption that the index is perfect or, if it is almost perfect, it only needs the tinkering of a skilled manager. Often, the manager believes he or she can get a better return without higher risk or a higher tracking error.

One way to change an index is through the management of industry sectors. A manager can reduce or eliminate stocks in sectors that he or she believes are overvalued, then increase the stocks that appear undervalued.

This method of enhancement involves more trading than in a normal index fund, which results in higher transaction costs. In addition, because of the extra work done by a manager to obtain better results, there are higher management fees.

SYNTHETIC ENHANCEMENTS

This type of enhancement is an odd one because it is essentially a stock index fund with no stocks in it. Managers create this type of index by combining a cash position with a derivative, which is a highly leveraged investment.

Derivatives are manufactured investments, such as futures, with a price that fluctuates based on the price of something else. For example, if an index price goes up, then the prices of that index's future contracts, and call options also go up. Because a derivative is leveraged, a large move in the derivative can occur with only a slight move in the index.

Derivatives — when managed correctly — can track a benchmark closely, and mutual fund managers will use them often to recreate synthetic index funds. An investor can beat the market by a small margin using index arbitrage, which is the capture of small differences that occur between the value of a derivative-based index, and the actual stock or bond market. It is not surprising that this method has become popular among investment management companies.

Managers also use a cash-plus strategy that is created using only future contracts, which require just a small down payment when purchased, called a margin. The rest of the cash can then be used to invest in other securities.

Option overwrite strategy allows managers to create and sell options against the actual securities in the fund. This often generates extra cash flow to the fund, but can limit the profit potential if the market moves up.

Consequently, enhanced index funds are often exposed to higher risks that go above the risks of the market. Normally, enhanced index funds should be left to those who have a strong understanding of them.

Leveraged Indexing

This type of index fund borrows extra money and puts it cash into stocks or bonds. The borrowing can be as much as 50 percent of the value of the fund in some scenarios. If the return on the portion of the index fund that is leveraged is higher than that of the cost to borrow, then the fund has made an extra return on the market. On the other hand, if it does not make up the borrowing costs, it performs below the market.

If interest rates drop and the stock market goes up, this is a "best case" for leveraged funds because borrowing costs are reduced and the fund makes extra return from its increased market position. The "worst-case" scenario for this is if interest rates go up and the market goes down; this will increase the interest costs but result in the fund sustaining losses because of the drop in the market. This type of indexing is extremely risky.

Inverse Indexing

The practice of selling stocks you do not own and buying them back at lower prices in the future is called inverse indexing. This is also called "shorting the market" because you make money if the stock market goes down. The difference between the sell price and buy-back price is the profit an investor earns.

Using derivatives will also allow investors in inverse index funds to earn money on a bad market because they will sell futures in an index, buy options on the index and then do an equity swap.

The last way that inverse indexing can work is by buying inverse index funds because they use derivatives that go in the opposite direction of the market. This, like leveraged indexing, is a highly risky type of investing.

Diversification

Someone diversified in the stock market has a number of different securities in a fund, which reduces the volatility of the market by decreasing the impact of large price swings on the average return of a single security. Essentially, do not place all your investment eggs in one basket. Do not put all your faith in the new company you heard about that is supposed going to skyrocket in the market and invest all of your money in it.

Not having much diversification can lead to an increased risk for an investor. Because large companies may fall in price, this could negatively affect the portfolio's value. By spreading out the risk, the returns can be greater for an investor that uses a diversified portfolio.

Stocks are unpredictable; not diversifying causes an investor to be subject to the rise and fall of that one stock. When investors put their investment into a concentrated focus, they increase the risk with little promise of higher returns.

There are several varieties of diversification, some of which we will outline here.

Horizontal Diversification

This type of diversification is when an investor diversifies between same-type investments, which can be a broad or narrow diversification, like investing in several New York Stock Exchange Companies or stocks of the same sector.

Vertical Diversification

Vertical diversification is the investment between various types of investments. It can be incredibly broad or incredibly narrow — much like horizontal diversification — and normally involves diversifying between bonds and stocks or diversifying between stocks of different branches. Horizontal diversification lessens the risk of investing all-in-one, but vertical diversification protects an investor against market and/or economical changes.

Super-Diversification

This is the highest degree of diversification, occurring when institutional asset class funds are used to construct a financial portfolio. This is a relatively new concept, with the term only coming into being in the book *Wealth Without Worry* by Jim Whiddon and Lance Alston in 2005. On average, this type of asset class portfolio holds between 10,000 and 12,000 securities through a smaller number of institutional asset class funds.

How Much Return Comes From Diversification?

Characteristically, all investment parts of diversification will be lower than the return of the top-performer-part, which is the price you pay for having lower-risk. Conversely, using various strategies to put more weight on a higher-risk stock in the portfolio, an investor could reap the benefits of the higher-risk.

Asset Allocation

This is defined as the process of determining the mix of stocks, bonds, and other classes of assets that match an investor's risk capacity. The risk capacity includes the investor's attitude toward risk, net income, net worth, knowledge about investing, and time horizon.

Research in the economics field has found asset allocation is an important factor in determining a portfolio's return. Asset allocation is often 100-percent responsible for the variance in an investment's performance.

An index fund is invested only in the fixed-income positions that make up an asset class. Therefore, it possesses the same rules, ownership, and expected performance of the comparable index.

A major aspect of financial planning is finding an asset allocation that matches a person's appetite for risk on the stock market, which can depend on several factors, including the investor's ability to shoulder risk.

The best-performing asset normally will vary depending on the year, and it is not easy to predict. There are several examples of asset classes: cash, bonds, stocks, real estate, and luxury collectibles. All of these can be broken down by size (Large-Cap, Mid-Cap, and Small-Cap), Style (Growth,

Blend, and Value), or into Real Estate Investment Trusts and international investments.

A study from 1986 by Brinson, Hood, and Beebower looked at asset allocation for 91 large pension funds measured from 1973 to 1985. The researchers replaced the pension funds' stock, bond, and cash selections with market indexes and the indexed returns; quarterly returns were found to be higher than the pension plan's actual quarterly return. A follow-up study was done in 1991, proving asset allocation can create greater returns for investors. Researchers found that replacing active picks with simple asset classes worked just as well as, if not better than, pension managers.

In 1997, William Jahnke created a debate on this topic by attacking the study in his paper, "The Asset Allocation Hoax," which appeared as an opinion piece in the *Journal of Financial Planning*. His main criticism was that be believed Brinson, Hood, and Beebower's use of quarterly data dampened the impact of compounding slight portfolio disparities over time, relative to the benchmark.

In 2000, Ibbotson and Kaplan used five asset classes — large-cap, small-cap, non-U.S. stock, U.S. bonds, and cash — in their study "Does Asset Allocation Policy Explain 40, 90, or 100 Percent of Performance?" After examining the ten-year period of 94 U.S. balanced mutual funds opposed to the indexed returns, they found actual returns failed to beat the index returns. They concluded it explained 40 percent of the variation of returns across funds and 100 percent of the level of fund returns; Brinson agreed with the conclusions presented.

When asset allocation planning is being done, there should be consideration made to the number of stocks and bonds in a portfolio. When buying stocks, an investor should consider the possibility of a bear market, which could result in panicked selling by investors. For example, during the bear market of 2000 to 2002, a portfolio with 80 percent stocks and 20 percent bonds would experience a -34.35 percent return on their investment. For a portfolio of 60 percent stocks and 40 percent bonds the return would be -19.99 percent. If investors had a portfolio of 40 percent stocks and 60 percent bonds, they would only suffer a -7.46 percent reduction in their return. Alternatively, if the investors' portfolio were made of 20 percent stocks and 80 percent bonds, the return would have actually increased by 6.29 percent.

Who is an Active Investor?

Most investors in the stock market are active investors. Even though research has shown that most investors cannot beat the market, 90 percent of investors' assets are actively managed in the stock market.

Active investors have the return objective of beating the market through stock, time, manager picking, and style drifting; these will be discussed again in Chapter 3.

Normally, the state of mind of an active investor is classified as stressed, and his or her net performance often is well below the index because of fees, expenses, taxes, and missed opportunities.

Active investors comprise almost all brokerage firms, mutual fund companies, market timing services, investment press, and brokerage training programs.

An effective way to understand active investors is to compare them to gamblers. Their style of investing often goes on a "gut feeling." Most active investors believe they have a special understanding of the market that others lack, which gives them an edge over everyone else. No different than gambling, active investing can be a hectic ride for investors that enjoy the feeling of excitement through risking it all on the chance of the stock market. At the same time, it can be devastating when the risk becomes too great — and they end up losing.

Often, active investors do not account for gains and losses, along with quoting the returns of only the portion of their portfolio that performed well. Investment returns often depend on the behavior of an investor, and active investors will make bad decisions when trying to outperform the market. During the 1980s and 1990s, when the stock market was rising, investors did well and started to believe that they could beat the market, which is actually impossible.

During a study in 1997, *Money Magazine* and the Vanguard Group selected 1,555 investors from across the country and asked them 20 questions on investing. The study found that the average mark for the 20 questions was 67 percent correct, while in 2000, an updated survey found only 37 percent of the respondent's questions were correct.

Short-term capital gains that occur from frequent trading of an active investor also have an unfavorable tax treatment when the funds are held in a taxable account. Overall, the majority of active investors in the United States have failed to outperform a passive stock index for several decades.

There is no magic eight ball to investing; there is no such thing as an infallible "gut feeling" on a stock; and there is no way to perfectly predict the future of the stock market. Like a gambler, when they are up, they think they are beating the system. But when things are down and they are in a dry spell, the claims of a prediction on future outcomes vanish as quickly as the profits they hold.

Who is an Index Fund Investor?

The approach of an index fund investor is often described as scientific, with investors analyzing decades of risk and return data to make measurements on the future performance of the market criteria.

Index fund investors also are less active, and there is a lower rate of stock selling and buying. Indexing, while still new — the first index fund came to fruition in 1971 — is a growing trend and accounts for 44 percent of the institutional assets currently invested in index funds.

Unlike years past, when it was considered an insult and un-American to invest in index funds, the trend has received new life through many high-profile supporters: Charles Schwab has 75 percent of his mutual fund investments in index funds; also, Warren Buffett, Barclays

Global Investors, Dimension Fund Advisors (DFA), and the Vanguard Group (who as we will see in the next chapter) have all been pioneers of the index fund movement since the mid-1970s.

Index funds are structured to provide the same performance as an index, and index fund investors are not trying to outperform the market. Index fund investors are, therefore, often called passive investors.

The rationale behind becoming an index fund investor stems from four concepts of financial economics.

1. The average investor, in the long term, will have an average performance equal to the average market. As a result, the investor will benefit more by reducing investment costs rather than trying to beat the market, as an active investor does.

2. Because of the efficient market hypothesis, which states that equilibrium in market prices fully reflects all the available information, it is just about impossible to beat the market through active investing.

3. There is also the principal-agent problem, in which the principal, or investor, allocates money to a manager or agent and must give the right incentives to the manager to ensure the manager runs the portfolio along the lines of the investor's risk and return goals. This is made much easier with index fund investing.

4. The Capital Asset Pricing Model implies that all investors when in equilibrium will hold a mixture of the market portfolio and no risk assets. Under suitable conditions, a fund indexed to the market is the only fund investors need.

Thanks to the bull market that existed in the 1990s, index investing skyrocketed because investors were able to achieve a desired and absolute return rate simply by having portfolios that benchmarked to broad-based indexes like the S&P 500, Russell 3000, or Wilshire 5000.

On a consistent basis, index fund managers have outperformed a majority of active managers while, at the same time, have lower fees and higher after-tax returns. Though an active manager may beat the index occasionally, sometimes for a period of a few years, the investor does not know if it was due to luck or skill, or if that success in the past will translate into bigger returns in the future.

Index fund investors can enjoy a relaxed state of mind because they are not pressured into beating anything, and they can approach the market by buying and holding globally diversified portfolios of index funds. This method of investing is supported by University of Chicago Nobel Prize winners.

What Would You Do?

Let us look at a scenario. You have $10,000 given to you through an inheritance or lottery. You realize this is your ticket to getting rich through investing in the stock market. "Why not?" you say. "Lots of people do it and they become wealthy, so why not me?"

You are presented with three options; Give your money to a stock picker; pick the stocks yourself; or go with an index fund.

Scenario One: The Stock Picker

Say you decide to go with a stock picker. With your $10,000, you decide to take the money you have been given and give it to someone else. But you are not actually giving the money to the stock picker; you are lending him the money hoping he will give you more money back. There is no guarantee you will get all or any of you money back in this scenario.

The stock picker has your money and he regales you with all the riches that will soon fall at your feet. As we will see in Chapter 3, stock pickers have no real science behind them, and they are often wrong. If they do gamble and win, it is out of luck — not out of skill. You have given your money to the stock picker and, a few months later, you find the stocks he invested in for you have fallen; that $10,000 is now only $3,000. Nevertheless, the stock picker tells you to stay strong and ride the dip, because "what goes down, must come up." What follows is months of agonizing over the loss of money, the fall of the stock, and the reassurances from the stock picker that things will change. Maybe they will, but the extra stress you experience from the rise and fall of the stock is certainly unpleasant.

Scenario Two: You Pick 'em!

You have your $10,000 and are ready to try your fortunes in the stock market, but you are not falling into the trap of a stock picker. This is your money, and you are going to take it and invest it on your own.

You buy all the books that tell you how to pick the winning stocks; you watch MSNBC to see what is rising and what is falling; you log on to your computer and begin investing in everything that suits your interest. You do not know which stocks will rise or which will fall, but you take the risk — it is your money, after all.

Days turn into weeks, weeks into months, and you have spent hours on end in front of the computer, contemplating what will happen with the stock. You pray to MSNBC to give you good news. You begin stressing if you will ever beat the market like the books said you would. You start to doubt if beating the market is even possible and whether you should keep attempting it.

You may decide to pull out while you are ahead and cut your losses, or you may decide to continue. These are dire predictions, and in actuality you could find that you do well with your stocks; you may make money.

Sadly, the odds are against you, and as we will see in Chapter 3, things do not always work out for those who pick their own stocks.

Scenario Three: Go with an Index Fund

You have finished counting your $10,000. Instead of choosing to invest in various stocks that you have heard good things about, or choosing to go with a stock picker with no more insight than you, you decide to try index funds.

Index funds, as you have read, are a streamlined way to take your money and improve on it. You know you most likely will not become significantly or instantly rich, but the small-term gains come with long-term benefits.

You will not be sitting in front of the computer hoping the stocks rise because you know you are not trying to beat the market, but rather, want to just replicate it. You will not worry about losing your money because you have diversified your portfolio over several stocks, industries, and even geographical areas. You will not worry about a bear market hitting because you have split up your stocks and your bonds to balance each other out.

Using the index fund route will not produce substantial amounts of money, but you will endure less stress; while your money may fall slightly, it could just as easily go up. You are not trying to beat the market here; you are replicating, mirroring, and reflecting it.

Now You Know

The next chapter will focus on the history of the index fund because, when we know the past, we can begin to understand the future. The history of the index fund goes back farther than the age of the United States. And, oddly enough, a method of investing in the stock market that takes the gamble out of the equation all started with a French gambler.

2

The History of the Index Fund

"History, insofar as it accustoms human beings to comprehend the whole of the past and to hasten forward with its conclusions into the far future, conceals the boundaries of birth and death, which enclose the life of the human being so narrowly and oppressively, and with a kind of optical illusion, expands his short existence into endless space, leading the individual imperceptibly over into humanity."

-Friedrich von Schiller-

To understand how the index fund can change your entire portfolio, then you should understand its evolution, where it came from, and why it took so long for such a revolutionary idea to take effect.

The history of the index fund stretches from the Renaissance, when its foundations were laid in an effort to gain more money gambling, through the industrial and digital revolutions, to our present day.

One would think that such a new concept would have sprung up sooner by a visionary who thought there had to be a better way to invest in the stock market. Yet the index fund needed different foundations to be cast before its true form could be realized. It took visionaries, gamblers, and those who questioned the status-quo to create the index fund as we know it.

The idea of index funds was not received well by many in the industry; one of the fathers of investing, Louis Bachelier, would suffer for it. As with most new ideas, it takes time for the establishment to come around, understand, and eventually accept it.

Decades after the idea of index funds began to take shape, the first index fund would be issued and, in a short quarter-century, the idea would become a revolution, changing the way stock market economics were conducted.

Let us travel back in time 450 years to a French gambler who was looking for a way to win more by improving his gambling chances.

Chevalier de Mere

To truly know the history of the index fund, we must revert to the year 1654, when French gambler Chevalier de Mere and his mathematician friend Blaise Pascal wanted to know the future to improve their gambling chances. Through their efforts to gain an advantage at games of chance, they created the Theory of Probability, which states that a future outcome will have an expected value depending on an average and a range of deviations from the average. This theory would prove to be the basis of modern finance and would be embraced years later by Harry Markowitz in landmark research, which will be discussed later.

Louis Bachelier

"Clearly the price considered most likely by the market is the true current price; if the market judged otherwise, it would quote not this price, but another price higher or lower."

– Louis Bachelier

In his doctoral thesis, *The Theory of Speculation*, Bachelier pioneered the concept of the Random Walk Theory and anticipated, in 1900, what would become the basis of future financial economic theories. The Random Walk Theory had three distinct rules: There needs to be a starting point in the walk; the distance between Point A and Point B needs to be constant; and the direction between the two points must be random with no direction more probable than another.

This paper would become the first to use advanced mathematics in the study of economics and finance. Sadly, his innovation was not appreciated at the time by his professors and peers, and his thesis received poor marks. He would shuttle between teaching jobs before settling in a small French town for much of his life.

The man who created the theories that comprise modern finance would not be fully recognized for his groundbreaking ideas until 1964 when MIT professor Paul Cootner published his research on randomness titled *The Random Character of Stock Market Prices*, which contained the translated text of Bachelier's thesis.

One interesting note about Bachelier's Random Walk Theory is that it predated by more than five years Einstein's study of Brownian motion, which is the random movement of particles suspended in fluids. Bachelier was ahead of his time.

The Random Walk Theory

How does a gambler and a man with a theory ahead of his time fit into index funds? Quite easily, thanks to the Random Walk Theory. The theory states that stock market prices evolve according to a random walk and, thus, cannot be predicted. This theory has been historically accepted by investors, economists, and financial behaviorists, but it has not stopped those adventurous few from trying to predict the stock market and beat it.

The Random Walk Theory of changing prices creates a notion among investors that stock prices change for no reason but, actually, they are random because the information that moves them is random. This theory would be improved upon by some of the individuals we will mention later in this chapter, including Burton Malkiel, who would write *A Random Walk Down Wall Street* in 1973.

Over time, this theory has also been applied to the National Basketball Association (NBA), with psychologists making a detailed study of every shot by the Philadelphia 76ers over the course of one and a half seasons; they found no correlation between the previous shots and the outcomes of the shot afterwards. This also applies to the stock market: If a stock goes up one day, no one can predict if it will rise the next, and the same is true for basketball. If a player makes a nice shot, it does not mean he will make another nice shot the next time.

Yet there are those who think the market is predictable to some degree. They believe there are trends and changes in the prices that you can look for to determine when the stock will rise or fall. There have even been books printed by economists and professors trying to prove the Random Walk Theory wrong. One of the men who does not buy into the theory is Martin Weber, a leading researcher of behavioral finance who did several tests on trends in the stock market. In observing the stock market over a period of ten years, he discovered that stocks with high-price increases in the first five years tended to become under performers in the next five years. Those who do not believe the Random Walk Theory cite this as an example of the how the theory is wrong. Despite this, ample evidence exists to prove that the Random Walk Theory is, indeed, how the market runs.

The Earliest Index

As stated in the previous chapter, the earliest index was the Dow Jones Industrial Average.

After the creation of the Dow Jones, little happened over the next quarter-century to pave the way for index funds until the outbreak of the first World War. It also was during this time that the United States began to make the switch from an agrarian economy to an industrial one, due to the fact that no factories in the United States were damaged by World War I. With the 1920s bull market thriving, new investment trusts were created that allowed individuals to participate in the market for as little as $100.

The investors pooled their money together with a trust company for the purpose of investing. Each investor was issued a certain number of shares that would represent how much money they had invested. Investors in the trust could then buy and sell shares on the stock market in the same way that stocks were traded.

Sadly, this practice also led to many small investors being defrauded of their money. Pools were established to attempt to monopolize an industry or to eliminate unwanted investments that investors hold. Banks were notorious for this practice during this time.

As a result, the open-end trust was created. It was different than traditional trusts in that it could only be invested in publicly available common stock that investors could track daily. The trust could not borrow money to leverage portfolio holdings, and shares could be redeemed by those in the trust at the net asset value of the day.

The first fund held a portfolio of 46 stocks and, within one year of its formation, there were three mutual funds available to investors: MIT, Putnam Investors, and State Street Investment Corporation. It was not long before researchers recognized the advantages a portfolio that focused on indexes provides. By 1933, Alfred Cowles published a report about Wall Street and the pointless need for research to beat the market. In his opinion, the market was far too complex for this. The Cowles Commission Index began, and it tracked all the stocks that traded on the New York Stock Exchange. In the 1960s, it would be reintroduced as the S&P 500 index.

The Cowles Commission

"Science is Measurement"

Cowles was the son and grandson of two major stockholders of the Chicago Tribune Company, and finance seemed to be in his blood. While dealing with a bout of tuberculosis in Colorado Springs, Colorado, when he was a young man, Cowles began to handle his family's finances. To know familiarize himself with the markets, Cowles received investment services to keep at the top of the game.

After the crash of 1929, Cowles became disillusioned with the markets and decided to help investors achieve a successful portfolio. To accomplish this, Cowles looked at more than 12,000 recommendations and four years of transactions by 20 leading fire insurance companies; this would prove the basis of a report published in 1933. He would publish a follow-up in 1944, reviewing the markets over a 15½-year time frame and, again, concluded that a forecaster could not predict the future of the market.

Before he published the follow-up report, Cowles created the Cowles Commission for Research in Economics in 1932 with the motto "science is measurement."

The commission moved to Chicago in 1939 and, basing itself out of the University of Chicago, turned the economics department of the university into a hotbed of research for decades to come. The commission later moved to Yale in 1955 and changed its name to the Cowles Foundation. One testament to the importance of the commission is that every winner of the Nobel Prize in economics in the United States has, at one time or another, spent time with the Cowles Commission or Foundation.

The Cowles Commission went on to create the S&P 500 Index. Cowles' goal in creating the index was to make a representation of the average experience of stock market investors. Despite his belief that the market could not be predicted, and the fact he produced countless items of research to back up the claim, Cowles believed investors would always look at market forecasters because they needed to believe that someone could predict the market's future.

Harry Markowitz

Born in Chicago on August 24, 1927, Harry Markowitz had a deep interest in physics and philosophy. These two interests would shape his future economic theories while he attended the University of Chicago.

In the early 1950s, Harry Markowitz was a graduate student in search of a thesis. After speaking with an advisor's stockbroker, he found the thesis he was looking for and started creating standard research reports published in the finance industry.

Markowitz was initially struck by the focus on return in the financial sector that seemed to be the primary consideration in choosing assets. He found that when portfolio managers analyzed the risk in an investment, they did not fully understand the relationships between securities. In his thesis, he described a way that a well-diversified portfolio reduced the risk of an equity investment.

In his classic paper, *Portfolio Selection*, which was published in 1952 while he was still attending the University of Chicago, he stated that the best portfolio provides investors with the optimal trade-off between return, and risk and investors should have many different portfolios because different people have varied risk tolerances.

In theory, a new investor with a long road ahead would invest in a portfolio that would offer high returns but come at a steep risk. On the flip side, an investor nearing retirement would take a low-risk, low-return portfolio.

This theory went against the belief that an investor would buy only a few firms that he or she had researched extensively. This would lay the first foundations for the index fund, which was still two decades away. The reason for the long delay between his paper and the first index fund came down to technology. Analyzing 100 security portfolios with 100 expected returns, 100 standard deviations, and 4,950 correlations was simply too much data to calculate at that time.

Later, Markowitz published a book titled *Portfolio Selection: Efficient Diversification of Investments*, which presents the theory that allows investors to understand the risk and return scenarios of investing in stocks. Markowitz developed a formulated, operational theory for portfolio selection under uncertainty.

Before Markowitz, risk was discussed in broad terms with little in the way of hard facts to back it up; risk was based on "gut feelings" rather than economics. Markowitz showed that an investor's portfolio choice could be reduced by balancing the expected return on the portfolio and the standard deviation. As a result, the risk of a portfolio with many stocks depended not only on the return of the various assets, but also the opposite movement of the assets.

In his book, he said, "Diversification is both observed and sensible. A rule of behavior that does not imply the superiority of diversification must be rejected both as a hypothesis and as a maxim."

While Markowitz put together his revolutionary economic theory, most investors were of the mindset that potential stock investors should put everything they had into the one stock they expected to perform the best. The rationale was that holding all your investments in one promising return on a stock would be exceedingly profitable. In other words, if you had only one stock, the chance of your losing was small, opposed to the chance of losing if you had many stocks.

Markowitz felt that risk was central to investing, and investors could not expect higher returns without taking higher risks. He found a way to create an investment portfolio, called the "efficient portfolio," which offered an investor the highest return for any level of risk, and low risk for any given return.

For his surprisingly simple theory, Markowitz won the Nobel Prize for economics in 1990.

James Tobin

"I studied economics and made it my career for two reasons: the subject was and is intellectually fascinating and challenging, particularly to someone with taste and talent for theoretical reasoning and quantitative analysis"

– James Tobin

Born on March 5, 1918, Tobin, an economist from Yale, agreed with Markowitz that there were several benefits to portfolio diversification. In his paper, *Liquidity Preference as Behavior Toward Risk*, Tobin focused on the separation theorem that claims Markowitz's theory of an efficient portfolio was separate from the choice to divide up the portfolio between risky and risk-free assets. According to Tobin, investors could choose between a wide variety of risks in their portfolio.

Tobin was a supporter of Keynesian economics and believed governments should intervene in the economy to stabilize output and avoid recessions. Through his work in economics and his role in the index fund revolution, Tobin was awarded the John Bates Clark Medal in 1955 — an award to an economist under the age of 40 that made the most significant contribution in economic thought and knowledge. He won the Nobel Prize in economics in 1981.

William Sharpe

"I asked the question that microeconomists are trained to ask: If everyone were to behave optimally, what prices will securities command once the capital market has reached equilibrium? The conclusion was both startling and provocative. Security prices will adjust until there is a simple linear relationship between expected return and sensitivity to changes in the factor in question. Following the conventions of regression analysis, I used the symbol beta for the latter. Thus the result could be succinctly stated: securities with higher betas will have higher expected returns. Only the portion of risk due to the influence of the common factor will be rewarded in the long run. No compensation is needed nor available for the remainder (which I termed 'nonsystematic risk') since it can be reduced to a small amount by sensible diversification; thus was the capital asset pricing model born."

–William Sharpe

Sharpe was born June 16, 1934. Upon entering college, he had planned for a career in medicine at the University of California in Berkeley. However, after changing universities and going to Los Angeles, Sharpe switched his career focus to economics. While at the University of California in Los Angeles, he learned of the theories of Markowitz. In 1956, he joined the RAND (Research and Development) Corporation and gained the chance to work with Markowitz. While he earned his Ph.D., Sharpe developed the theory of Capital Asset Pricing Models, which states that the uncertainty of stock returns is caused by both unsystematic and systematic risk factors.

Several economists worked on the Capital Asset Pricing Models, but Sharpe's essay, *Capital Asset Prices: A Theory of Market Equilibrium under Conditions of Risk*, published in 1964, especially stands out.

Systematic risk comes from an investor simply going with the stock market, which includes an unexpected rise in inflation. Unsystematic risk is tied to a certain stock that includes rumors of management changes or product recalls.

Sharpe stated systematic risk should be rewarded because the investor is exposed to the economy as a whole. Unsystematic risk is simply a particular set of shares in which one or more companies is not susceptible to as much risk as systematic risk and, therefore, should not be rewarded.

One of the Sharpe's pioneering innovations was the Sharpe Ratio, which is used for risk-adjusted investment performance analysis and has contributed to the development of the binomial method for the variation of options, asset allocation optimization, and returns-based analysis in investment funds.

Capital Asset Pricing Models have become the backbone of modern price theory in finance. These models are used for empirical analysis and practical economic research, and are an important decision-making tool in a variety of areas.

Sharpe won the Nobel Prize for economics in 1990 for his theories.

Eugene Fama

"The bond market is a simpler market than the stock market. Bonds are simpler to evaluate than stocks because there's downside risk, but you don't have to worry much about the upside: They're not going to pay you more than they promised. So bonds are much simpler to deal with."

– Eugene Fama

Born on Valentine's Day in 1939, Eugene Fama would shake up the world of Wall Street through a revolutionary theory based on Markowitz's work that proved investing was a game of randomness.

Fama, another graduate of the department of economics at the University of Chicago, would become the next pillar of modern finance and index fund investing. Fama built upon the ideas of Bachelier, Cowles, and Samuelson to create a comprehensive theory that would explain why the stock market was so random and fluctuated so much.

While working on a stock market newsletter as an undergraduate at Tufts University, Fama had to find, buy, and sell signals based on certain market trends. What he discovered would show him the high degree that the market could fluctuate and the randomness that existed in it.

After graduating from the University of Chicago, Fama began teaching there, basing his lectures on the theories of Harry Markowitz. Markowitz's theories were unknown at the time, and Fama was the first to bring them to the attention of the finance department.

In January 1965, Fama published his 105-page dissertation, *The Behavior of Stock-Market Prices.* He theorized that major brokerage firms have large resources to analyze industry trends, interest rates, and accounting data, enabling them to regularly outperform a randomly selected portfolio of securities that have the same risk. He concluded that analysts inconsistently outperform the market: Even if he or she has no skills, analysts have a 50 percent chance of outperforming a random selection.

With an article published in the *Journal of Finance,* Fama created the theory of the efficient market hypothesis in 1970, which he stated had weak, semi-strong, and strong levels. The weak level constituted a past price behavior incorporated into stock prices, while the semi-strong level reflected current information such as earning reports. In the strong level, it was not possible to benefit from monopolistic information, defined as information from every source that has the ability to translate itself into valuable asset selections.

Fama believed that inexpensive stock information is available to everyone and the available information is reflected in the current stock price. This is because the price agreed upon by a seller and buyer is the best estimate of the value of a stock. Because stock prices can change in an instant, Fama thought it was risky and nearly impossible to capture returns in excess of the market returns. His research was later summarized in an article called "Random Walks in Stock Market Prices" by *The Financial Analysts Journal.*

The theory states that individuals cannot beat the stock price due to all the available information on the stock, which have already become a part of the stock price. It was not well-received by those who thought they could anticipate fluctuations in a stock price.

A famous example of this philosophy occurred in 1968 at the Institutional Investor Conference, when a manager stated that his career amounted to more than just throwing darts at *The Wall Street Journal*. In 1992, ABC news reporter John Stossel used this comment to illustrate a point. He threw darts at *The Wall Street Journal* to select stocks and then monitored their performances. Stossel's "dart choices" outperformed 90 percent of the Wall Street experts' stocks, and the "Random Walk" theory began to take hold.

Michael Jensen

A graduate student of Fama's, Jensen published the next great theory in the evolution of index funds. His paper, *The Performance of Mutual Funds in the Period of 1945-1964*, was the first to study actively managed mutual funds to learn professionals' failures in outperforming market indexes.

Using Sharpe's volatility measure as a beta test, Jensen added a risk dimension that incorporated the idea that investors who take more risk get a higher return. Jensen found if an investor held a broad portfolio of common stocks — all at the same risk level as mutual funds — they could, in theory, earn up to 15 percent more. In the study, only 26 of 115 funds outperformed the market, showing that fund managers have access to a great deal of research, contacts, and associations that allow them to become experts with indexes. This created a question: If experts cannot beat an index, who can?

The Foundation Is Set

Due to the foundation work of these few men, the academic community began to debate which level of efficiency applied to stock prices. As is often the case, the business world ignored the coming revolution.

With the emergence of the bull market in the 1960s, willing professionals were able to find stocks that could outperform the market. But it was not until the bear market that followed that professionals started to differentiate between luck and skill. It was at this point that many realized that the market is so efficient, there is no use exploiting the inefficiencies.

Efficient Market Hypothesis

In this section, we will go into deeper detail about the efficient market hypothesis. Essentially, Louis Bachelier first developed the efficient process, noted in his paper *The Theory of Speculation*, but it was ignored until the 1950s.

After publishing his dissertation on the concept in 1965, Eugene Fama published a review of both the theory and the evidence in the hypothesis in 1970. He extended the paper and refined the theory when he added the three definitions of market efficiency: weak, semi-strong, and strong.

The efficient market hypothesis was tied to index funds because the market cannot outperform itself, and investors will always earn market returns minus their costs. The more active the investor is, the more transactions, market returns, and tax costs will rise for them. This was combined with the efficient market hypothesis' basic theory to ensure that the future earning potential of the macroeconomic picture had to be priced into the current value of the stock. Active investors felt they had to overcome higher costs, but the efficient market hypothesis stated it is not possible to understand the long-term movements of the market.

From this belief came the core philosophy of index-based investing. Because the market is so efficient, the best course of action when investing is to first take control of the controllable variables, thereby dampening risk through diversification and minimizing turnover, transaction costs, and taxes. Meeting these goals is the logic of index investing. Because of the diversification of an asset class, the low turnover, and low-cost tax efficiency, passive investors have a diverse array of index products.

Despite these benefits to index investing, the investing circles delayed the launch of index investing due to unfamiliarity with the intellectual concepts. When they did launch, it took many years to gain assets.

The First Index Fund

After years of academic debating, the first index fund was launched on July 1, 1971, by Wells Fargo, with a $6 million contribution from the Samsonite Corporation. Wells Fargo based the fund on an equal- weighted New York Stock Exchange. The launch of the first index fund was credited to another alumni of the University of Chicago Department of Economics, Charles Shwayder, the son of the head of the Samsonite Corporation. He was believed in the basic theory of index funds and was eager to launch the world's first index fund with Bill Fouse and John McQuown, who had joined the Wells Fargo Bank Management Science Division in 1964.

McQuown had a degree in mechanical engineering, but he had become interested in using computers on the stock market. The fund, which held an equal proportion of assets of each of the stocks listed on the New York Stock Exchange, proved to be a difficult experience to maintain. Because the return of each stock was unique and different than that of the other stocks, the portfolio had to be constantly rebalanced, with winners sold and losers purchased.

The excessive transaction costs of the strategy resulted in the equal-weighted theory being scrapped in favor of a market capitalization weighted fund. In this case — as long as dividends were reinvested — the fund grew automatically with market performance and required no rebalancing.

Two years after launching the first index fund, Wells Fargo followed up with the creation of the Stagecoach Fund, a market-weighted, closed-end mutual fund that tracked the S&P 500. It has since become a model for all index funds.

In 1973, two more University of Chicago Department of Economics graduates, David Booth and Rex Sinquefield, who had worked with Wells Fargo on the first index funds, created the American National Bank of Chicago, the first publicly marketed index fund based on the S&P 500 index. Ten years after graduating from university, Booth and Sinquefield teamed up again to create their own company. They founded the Dimensional Fund Advisors, which documented the return of small-cap stocks and was superior to that of large-cap stocks by 3 percent annually.

The basic investment philosophy of Dimension Fund Advisors was created from a paper written by three more University of Chicago Department of Economics graduates: Fama, Ken French, and Robert McCormick. They created the new investment policy of the Dimension Fund Advisors and put the academic theory into practice by outlining a three-factor investment policy — risk, size, and financial health — that determined the returns on stocks.

The timing was right for the index fund revolution to begin. Stock prices in 1974, adjusted for inflation, were at the same level as prices in 1954, and active funds were crashing under the pressure of a long, drawn-out bear market. Consequently, index funds rose in value from the initial $6 million in 1971 to more $10 billion by 1980.

Also assisting the process was the deregulation of the stock commission on May 1, 1975. Before this, the commission had 2 percent of the trade, which was a strong influence on indexing because indexed portfolios held a large number of stocks. As a result of the decommission, prudence in mutual funds would now be determined on the basis of diversification, as opposed to the examination of individual stocks.

Before the decommissioning, fund managers could not negotiate lower trading costs with brokers. Because index funds use a great deal of small trades, high commission would not work.

For much of the twentieth century, stockbrokers were paid 8 percent commission or more on mutual funds that were distributed through them; therefore, the mutual fund industry did not accept the idea of index funds with lower commissions.

Fund company executives also wanted to prove that their firm could beat the market, and any talk of index funds was a personal attack against them. Regardless of the increased revenue of indexing, it was Burton Malkiel's book, *A Random Walk Down Wall Street*, that put the academic research of indexing into a language that laypeople and investors could understand. Malkiel is credited with introducing the public to market efficiency, as well as market risk and return, because of his main point: The stock market is random and unpredictable in the short term due to the release of new information that can have a great influence on stock prices. He concluded that stock picking and an actively managed mutual fund portfolio are wastes of an investor's time when inexpensive and diversified index funds are available for long-term investors.

The next big wave in the index fund revolution began when Charles Ellis wrote an article called *The Loser's Game* in 1975. The article detailed how 85 percent of active managers failed to beat the S&P 500 index over ten years. He argued that investors can earn only the market's return, and for every loser there must be a winner — not all investors can outperform the market. Ellis suggested they should not try to outguess the market and should reflect the market at the lowest cost through passive index funds.

One year later, John Bogle, the man who would become known as Saint Jack for doing more with his dedication for the good of the investors than any other person in modern finance, issued the first index fund for investors.

John Bogle

"The courage to press on regardless—regardless of whether we face calm seas or rough seas, and especially when the market storms howl around us—is the quintessential attribute of the successful investor."

– John Bogle

Known as Saint Jack, Bogle was the head of the Vanguard Group, which introduced the first index fund for individual investors after being influenced by Malkiel's book. It all began in 1950 when Bogle was in Boston reading *Big Money*, which highlighted the expanding mutual fund industry.

Over the next 18 months, Bogle researched the mutual fund industry and wrote *The Economic Role of the Investment Company*, a 100-page thesis covering the dynamics and history of funds. In it, he made recommendations to fund companies to help them increase their sales, saying they needed to state a fund's objective and make no claim to superiority over the market averages.

It was not until 1975 that Bogle had the chance to put his theory into practice as the chairman of the Vanguard Group, the first company to offer index funds to the public at a low cost.

In May 1976, the Vanguard Group approved an index-fund style mutual fund and filed it with the U.S. Securities and Exchange Commission. It was approved as the First Index Investment Trust with an opening date of August 31, 1976. The Vanguard Group then began to explore how to support the fund through investments from large brokerage firms. Bogle set a goal of raising $50 to $150 million before the opening.

Commission on the fund was only 6 percent and, as a result of the lower commission, just $11.4 million was raised for the fund before opening day, and Vanguard was forced to cut ties with the brokerage firms that acted as a sales force. In 1980, they changed their name to the Vanguard 500 Index Fund.

Initial feelings about the venture were that Bogle had made a huge mistake, and it was labeled "Bogle's Folly." Many investors thought the idea would never catch on because of the average returns it provided. Yet despite a rough start, the Vanguard 500 Index Fund is now worth $110 billion.

Seven years later, Wells Fargo launched the next low-cost index fund, the Stagecoach Corporate Stock Fund. The fund was doomed from the start, with only a 1 percent management fee, and it did not survive the market.

Still, the index revolution could not be stopped. By 1986, nine more index funds were offered by various companies, although two of the funds were for obscure international markets, and a third fund was so expensive that it was out of business by 1993. But there were more success stories. The Vanguard Bond Market Fund, offered in 1986, benchmarked the Lehman Brothers Aggregate Bond Index. This bond would be the first to be used completely for the bond market. With a fee of only .25 percent per year, it is now worth $11 billion in assets.

Vanguard added a third index fund in 1987. The Extended Market fund, which was designed to benchmark the Wilshire 4500, invested in 2,000 of the largest companies on the index and 800 smaller ones. They added to it once more with index funds to benchmark the Russell 2000 Small-Cap, Morgan Stanley, and Pacific Basin indexes.

The new funds kept coming. Fidelity also started two index funds that benchmarked the Lehman Brothers Aggregate Bond and the S&P 500 indexes in 1990. Things truly started to take hold in the first year of the 1990s and, by the end of the year, there were 43 index funds available from several mutual fund companies. However, most of these funds had little capital, making Vanguard the clear leader, with nine index funds and assets worth $5 billion. But Vanguard would not stop with nine, adding 20 more over the course of the 1990s.

The '90s would prove to be a booming time for the index fund revolution. In 1990, 43 funds existed; by the end of 1999, there were 272. A total of 40 index funds were benchmarked for the S&P 500 index between 1997 and 1999 alone. By 2007, there would be more than 500 index funds available to the public, worth in excess of $1 trillion and taking up about 25 percent of the money invested in all mutual funds.

Burton G. Malkiel

"The sad truth is that there are only three kinds of financial prognosticators: those who do not know, those who do not know they don't know, and those who know they don't know but who get paid big buck to pretend they know."

– Burton G. Malkiel

Malkiel, born on August 28, 1932, redefined the index fund industry and become a leading supporter of the efficient market hypothesis. When the time came for someone to define index funding investment benefits and why it made sense for investors to pursue them, Malkiel was there with his book, *A Random Walk Down Wall Street*. Published in 1973, it laid out the principles of all the academic research conducted in the field by those before him.

Malkiel conducted an innovative test with his students by giving them a hypothetical stock initially worth $50. The closing price of the stock was determined by a coin flip. If it landed on "heads," the price would close half a point higher; if it landed on "tails," it would close half a point lower. Essentially, there was a 50-50 chance that the stock would close higher or lower than it did on the previous day. The test allowed Malkiel to determine trends, which he placed into a graph and took to a chartist, who predict future movements by looking at past patterns.

After examining the graph, the chartist told Malkiel to buy the stock. Malkiel replied that the results were from merely flipping a coin, proving that the markets and stocks were just as random as flipping a coin.

Through his book, Malkiel helped the private investor understand index funds, detailing why the time was right for index funds to be sponsored. Taking a cue from the book, the Vanguard Group created the First Index Investment Trust a few years after it was published. In 1977, the Vanguard Group made Malkiel a member of their board of directors. He has since been a member of the Council of Economic Advisors, president of the American Finance Association, and dean of the Yale School of Management.

In 1977, Malkiel wrote an article for the *Journal of Finance* titled "The Valuation of Closed-End Investment Company Shares" that questions why closed-end fund companies trade at market valuations lower than the net value of their assets. In the article, he raised a question: If the net asset value and market capitalization are both ways of measuring the same thing, then why is there a consistent difference between them? He did not believe the discount was due to management fees, as had been theorized before, because fees remain constant and do not explain the changes in the discount size during the life cycle of the fund.

David Booth

The University of Chicago's Department of Economics is renowned for the number of financial geniuses who have come out of its halls, with many aspiring economists paving the way for the index fund revolution. David Booth, a student in that department, was no different. He learned how the stock market worked as a student of a founder of the index fund revolution, Eugene Fama, whose principles he would take into the world of finance upon his graduation in 1971.

Although a great deal of research existed, Booth thought investors still did not understand how market efficiency worked. He read as much as he could from previous decades of research in the index field, which he believed gave investors an advantage, and to explore the frontiers of investing, Booth set up a Quotron machine in his apartment with Rex Sinquefield. In 1981, he founded Dimensional Fund Advisors (DFA). Booth was one of the first in the investment community to run with the idea of equilibrium and believe that scientific methods prove there is a relationship between risk and return. By December 2006, DFA was worth $123 billion.

Dimensional Fund Advisors

Created in 1981 by David Booth and Rex Sinquefield, DFA is based on the research done by Eugene Fama and Kenneth French. With headquarters in Santa Monica, California, the company now boasts thousands of employees worldwide. The employees, board members, and some outside investors own the company, including Arnold Schwarzenegger. Two board members on DFA include Nobel Laureates Myron Scholes and Robert C. Merton.

DFA manages more than $155 billion of funds as of 2006, but funds are not offered to the public directly. Instead, they are available through institutional investors and registered investment advisors.

The advisors have the goal of delivering the performance of capital markets and adding value through the design and trading of portfolios. The firm does not follow the usual rules and rigidity of traditional index funds by avoiding the cost-generating activity of stock pricing and market timing. Instead, DFA looks at the dimensions of capital markets that reward investors. DFA investment strategies deliberately target specific risk factors and create a diverse and well-designed total index portfolio.

The University of Chicago

As of 2004, 23 Nobel Laureates in Economics attended or taught at the University of Chicago, making up almost half of all the Nobel Laureates in Economics in history. The next closest to reach that level of prestige is Harvard, which is associated with four Nobel Laureates in Economics.

University of Chicago's economic reputation is due in no small part to Louis Engel, who served as vice-president of Merrill Lynch. In 1959, he called James Lorie at the university to learn how most people performed in the stock market. Lorie was so intrigued by the question that he set up a project to gather prices, dividends, and rates of return on all stocks listed. The ultimate goal was to create an accurate database so researchers did not have to compile their own data. In 1960, the Center for Research in Security Prices at the University of Chicago Booth School of Business was created with help from a $300,000 grant from Merrill Lynch to house the computer needed for the project. Support has been high for the program, and from 1964 to 1986, the center received more than $1 million from donors.

The stock market database was completed in 1964 after nearly three million pieces of information had been entered. This allowed Lorie and Fisher to look at total return, dividends received, and other factors that changed stock market prices between 1926 and 1965. They found that the average rate of return on the New York Stock Exchange was 9 percent.

A Long and Winding Road

Few could have guessed that more than 400 years ago, a gambler would spark a slow revolution that would change the world of finance forever. Of course, that revolution took a long and winding road to reach its current state, thanks to the many who saw that the system could be improved and did what they could to make it happen.

But it was not all happy endings and Nobel prizes. In spite of creating a revolutionary theory that predated Einstein, Louis Bachelier was too ahead of his time. What should have been a Nobel prize-winning paper would have been entirely lost to history were it not for a few people like Markowitz, who took up the torch and continued to develop the theory.

From the Random Walk Theory came the foundations of the index fund. Students at the University of Chicago questioned the concept of the stock market, wondering what can be done even if the stock market is unpredictable. From that question came the idea of neither trying to predict how the market would move, nor beating it as a result, but merely replicating it. Thus, the concept of the index fund was born through the minds of those future Nobel prize winners.

Instead of losing the idea to history, questions continued to be asked. The revolution moved forward through the 1960s thanks to Eugene Fama, who took the next step in the evolution by proving that the stock market is so efficient, there is no way to predict it. Rather than beat that efficiency, Fama recommended simply moving with it.

Then came the 1970s, when starting index funds became mainstream. It was a rocky start, but they moved ahead and began to be accepted through the 1980s. But with the arrival of the'90s, the finance world changed dramatically, and the concept of the index fund finally took off. Throughout that decade, index funds increased in magnitude, and by the middle of the first decade of the 2000s, more than 500 existed.

3

Why Index Funds Are the Way to Go

"Everyone has the obligation to ponder well his own specific traits of character. He must also regulate them adequately and not wonder whether someone else's traits might suit him better. The more definitely his own a man's character is, the better it fits him."

-Marcus Tullius Cicero

Index funds have advantages that include the ease of risk budgeting, low fees, and simplicity, and they have historically outperformed other indexes. Their low risk compared to other types of investments make them one of the best ways investors can take part in the stock market without risking everything they own on it.

It is true that the rewards can be small and slow-going, but there is no such thing as getting rich quick, so investors best not try.

Advantages of Using Index Funds

Ease of Risk Budgeting

Index fund investing offers the ease of risk budgeting. This means that the degree of difference from the benchmark is related to the number and size of bets the manager makes. Indexing also provides pension-plan sponsors with new techniques for eliminating holes that generate risk in a portfolio grouped through index accounts.

Low Fees

Note that there are rather low fees and costs in index fund investing. The fees of other managers are much higher than that of an index fund manager because index funds have fewer underlying costs. Active managers normally have more portfolio turnover because they are constantly acting on their investment and incur higher turnover-related costs. This is in contrast to index managers, who realign portfolio composition only to reflect index changes. In a tax-sensitive portfolio, this helps to avoid the recognition of investment gains.

Composition

Because the composition of a target index is a known quantity, it costs less to run an index fund. There are no highly paid stock pickers or analysts needed for this, and expense rations of an index fund range between .15 percent for U.S. Large Company Indexes to .97 percent for Emerging Market Indexes.

As of 2005 the average large-cap, actively managed mutual fund was 1.36 percent. Therefore, if a mutual fund produced 10 percent return before expenses — taking into account the expense ration difference — it would create an after-expense return of 9.85 percent for an index fund, but only 8.64 percent for an actively managed mutual-cap fund. And it should be noted the investment costs for active funds have increased over the past decade while index funds have decreased.

And there are crossing opportunities that provide savings for a plan sponsor. Crossing matches buyers to sellers, either within a firm or through industry-developed crossing networks, which help to save both the buyer and seller a bid/offer spread. Securities crossing has also become an important tool in index portfolios. Frequently, index-based managers have an advantage over traditional active managers who do not access the crossing. The savings generated from association with security transactions are often higher than their own management fees.

Simplicity

Choosing managers for index fund investing is relatively easy because indexing eliminates several criteria in the search for managers of investment mandates. Active managers might pursue a wide range of asset selection, but index managers do not require the same degree of scrutiny in their investment process.

Investment objectives of index funds are also easy to understand. Once an investor knows the target index of an index fund, the securities that the fund holds can be determined more easily.

Furthermore, managing an index fund's holdings may require rebalancing only every six months to every year. This is in contrast to active investors who must continuously spend enormous amounts of time reading investment newsletters and financial reports, magazines, and other related news.

Lower Turnovers

Turnover is the selling and buying of securities by a fund manager, resulting in a capital gains tax charge that is often passed on to the fund investors. Because index funds are passive investments, the turnover is lower than those associated with active fund investors. This keeps taxes low and makes a difference in the pre-tax and after-tax performance of an index fund.

Managers of active mutual funds often manage the money as if the taxes are only secondary — which is quite the contrary. Taxes can have a negative impact on the performance of an investment portfolio. A study conducted by John Bogle found that over a 16-year period, investors kept just 47 percent of their return in an average, actively managed mutual fund. Conversely, in a market index fund, they were able to keep 87 percent of the return.

No Style Drift

This occurs when actively managed mutual funds go outside their mid-cap value to increase returns. This can hurt portfolios that set diversification as a high priority. But this drift is not possible with an index fund and, therefore, an accurate diversification of a portfolio is increased.

Index Funds: Like a Mutual Fund, Only Better

An index fund allows enjoyment of the best parts of a mutual fund with little of the bad through buying stock in all the companies of an index, resulting in a reproduction of the performance of an entire section of the market. Index funds can perform much better than actively managed funds.

Investors are surprised when most mutual funds flop. For example, 85 percent of mutual funds that were set up to beat the S&P 500 in 1998 failed to meet that goal. But again — investing in a stock index fund means never outperforming the overall market.

The fact that 80 percent of mutual fund managers failed to achieve the goal of beating the market shows that while, in theory, it may seem easy to beat the market, in actuality, it is exceedingly hard. Even if a mutual fund does have a promising year, it could likely under perform the next. Index funds do not suffer from this.

The Folly of Active Investors

Active investors speak frequently about "beating the market." But as is evident, this is risky and nearly impossible to do. Not surprisingly, the effort to beat the market and become a big name on Wall Street has resulted in more than 90 percent of investors becoming active investors.

When buying into the myth that they can know the future movements of the market, investors will often gamble with others' money. If they succeed, they can be perceived as financial geniuses, and if they fail, they might blame it on the fluctuations of the market. New investors may dive into investing with a gung-ho attitude and the belief they will become rich quick through well-placed stock investing. This folly has become especially true with the advent of the Internet and online trading, through which anyone with a credit card and an Internet connection can buy and sell stocks online.

Active investors can be considered gamblers in disguise. Investing can turn into an addiction that can cost them everything, much like playing roulette can. Those in the financial world cannot forget the components of the efficient market theory: that the market is too efficient to beat, that information about stocks is widely available and, therefore, all known material and information is already reflected in stock prices. The price of a stock is the true value, determined by what a buyer wants and what a seller wants, and stock prices change too quickly to predict.

Even the man called the father of fundamental stock analysis, Benjamin Graham, says that investors cannot expect to beat the market.

The Folly of Stock Pickers

Stock pickers are similar to active investors: They bet they can beat the market by picking the stocks they expect to rise above the rest, and overall it is a game of chance that involves winning and losing.

Studies have shown it can take up to 20 years of stock picking to determine if one is skilled or just lucky, and it is almost impossible for a stock picker to consistently beat the long-term market. Stock pickers often fail because stocks are moved by daily news, which is, of course, unpredictable.

In 1993, Robert Jeffrey and Robert Arnott published the study *Is Your Alpha Big Enough to Cover its Taxes?.* They looked at 71 active mutual fund managers over a ten-year period, between 1982 and 1991, on the S&P 500. Most invested in styles that were similar to the S&P 500, but none were exact, and only two of the 71 managers beat the index. And John Bogle's study on stock pickers, *Bogle on Equity Fund Selection*, determined that only nine of 355 equity funds actually beat the benchmark over a period of 30 years.

Another study that revealed the failures of stock pickers was done by Walter Good and Roy Hermanson in a coin-flipping experiment. They asked 300 college students to guess the outcome of ten coin tosses, which were recorded and compared with the performances of 300 mutual fund managers over the course of ten years on the Morningstar® Principia®, a primary mutual fund database. The results showed that the students' guesses and the mutual fund managers' performance mirrored each other almost exactly, proving that stock picking is not a science — it is a guessing game. Stock pickers focus only on the short-term prospects and rarely look at the long-term market or its history.

The problem is clear in the case of Jack Grubman, who was considered the king of the telecom industry during the 1990s and the most influential power broker in the industry. He was also rated the top man in investor analyst rankings, with a power was so widespread that when he told people to buy or sell, they did it. He made $20 million a year and gave advice on 40 stocks with a market value of $1 trillion.

But in what is now well-known history, the telecom industry rose to amazing heights, then crashed and burned at the turn of the century. By March 2001, Grubman's top ten picks were at their lowest levels of the year; a year from then, half of the top ten companies he had listed were trading at $1 a share, with three filing for bankruptcy. Millions were lost by those who relied on Grubman's advice.

The Folly of Time Pickers

Time pickers are investors that think they can predict the future direction of the market, investing in stocks when the market is up and sheltering their investments in cash or bonds when the market is going down.

A landmark study of time pickers was conducted by John Graham of the University of Utah and Campbell Harvey of Duke University. The two men analyzed 15,000 predictions from 237 market timing investment newsletters from 1980 to 1992. Of the 237 newsletters that specialized in market-timing investment, 94.5 percent had gone out of business. The professors found that there was no evidence the newsletters could predict the future direction of the market, proving that the signals of the market cannot be predicted by time pickers.

Time pickers go against the notion of the Random Walk Theory, which states that the market cannot be predicted. Yet time pickers seem to be fooled by randomness, although nearly every academic study of the past 100 years has found that time picking is not an accurate way to play the stock market.

The SEI Corporation completed a study in 1992 that concluded that for a time picker to equal the average return of the stock market between 1901 and 1990, which was 9.5 percent, they would have to correctly select 70 percent of the ups and downs of the market. Even if time pickers called 100 percent of the declining markets and half of the rising markets, they would not exceed the return of the overall market during the same period.

Countless academic studies prove that time picking simply does not work and, more often than not, it generates negative returns for investors. But time-picking gurus still believe they can predict the future.

SmartMoney®, **www.smartmoney.com**, has analyzed and tracked time picker averages since 1997 and has found that of the top 11, their combined average is only 16 percent, with none of them performing above 23 percent. It is understood by economists that gains and losses are impossible to predict.

Time pickers also pay more in taxes. Some charge their clients 2 to 3 percent of the value of their investment portfolio but, in reality, time pickers are often well-paid gamblers who risk others' money. Time picking benefits financial firms that make money trading shares on poor advice from time picking "experts."

John Bogle, a giant in the index fund movement, has said that in 30 years, he has never seen anyone do market timing successfully or consistently. Time pickers have just two decisions to make: when to get into the market, and when to get out. The data shows that there is no reliable timing method to help make those decisions.

The Folly of Manager Pickers

The belief that one can select a manager who will be the perfect fit and make a client rich is a myth. There may be many managers out there under the illusion that they can beat the market, yet the number that can is near, if not at, zero.

Like any gambler, some managers can win occasionally, but usually they will lose — and take your money with them.

Investors might invest in the best mutual fund run by the best manager without realizing that today's top ten mutual funds often tank within a few years. Just because a manager did exceptionally well once does not guarantee it will happen again.

Experts cite that any outstanding track record of an investor is often a result of the manager benefiting from a market that, for a time, mirrored their management style. Thus, the performance of the manager is unpredictable and tied only to the will of the market. Excellent performance might occur when the mutual fund is small because the performance of the early fund will fuel growth in the fund in the form of investors' money.

Trying to predict the future performance of a mutual fund manager is like trying to pick stocks: It is next to impossible. A mutual fund manager can go from top to bottom within one year. In 2005, the ProFunds Ultra Japan Investment was managed by Petit/Banke/Joshi/Ames/Croll, who were the top managers that year; in 2006, they fell to 2,337th. Of the top ten managers in 2005, only one stayed in the top ten in 2006 (who fell from second to seventh), while half of the managers fell to and beyond 2,500th place.

Funds are unstable, and when they are hot, they are hot for only a short time. Numerous studies have shown that most mutual fund managers will do well one year and under perform in subsequent years. Having a hot mutual fund can even end up hurting you in the future, as "hot" does not always mean a cash influx.

In a 2005 report by John Waggoner of *USA Today*, it was reported that Fidelity Aggressive Growth Fund had $23 billion in assets in March 2000. Of that $23 billion, 65 percent comprised funds that investors had poured into the fund in the 12 months before the S&P 500 peaked in March 2000. In other words, a $10,000 investment in March 2000 would not be worth even $2,697 in April 2005. In the 12 months before the market peaked in 2000, investors put $228 billion into the 50 best-selling stock funds. Only two of those 50 actually gained over the next five years, and not even by much: 2.3 percent and 1.5 percent.

The common misconception among investors, helped in no small part by mutual fund advertisements, is that the fund did well in the past and will do so in the future. We know now that it is impossible to predict how a fund will perform in the future. Investors often go with mutual funds because they outperform index funds, but they do not take into account the higher risk generated by using a mutual fund manager. A manager with a good performance has likely taken money and concentrated it in specific stocks and bonds, and if it pays off, people will see it as a brilliant investment without understanding the risk involved.

The Silent Partners of Other Investments

Though not always realized, returns may have partners that many did not even know existed. These silent partners can include fees, expenses, taxes, and inflation. In total, they can equal more than half of a gross return. But by investing in index funds, the only uncontrollable partner will be inflation.

Silent partners can come in the form of:

- Sales agents or stockbrokers
- Income tax agencies
- Fund managers
- Accountants

- Firms that charge an advisory fee
- Market makers or transfer agents
- Mutual fund distributors
- Brokerage firms that earn interest on accounts

A study by John Bogle found that over a 15-year period, investors kept only 47 percent of their return. However, they could have kept 87 percent of that return if it had been in an index fund, which are tax efficient and, resultingly, have little to lose to the government. Tax-managed index funds make an index fund investment efficient by offsetting realized gains against realized losses, then deferring the realization of net capital gains and minimizing the dividend income.

A telephone survey by Dreyfus Corporation found that while 85 percent of mutual fund investors believed taxes played an important part in investment decision, only 33 percent believed they were knowledgeable in the tax implications of investing.

Active fund managers often manage pension plans and other tax-free items to avoid concern about tax implications. As a result, many managers of active funds disregard high taxes generated by their stock picks. But taxes do matter, and an index fund manager can minimize portfolio turnover, thereby maximizing unrealized capital gain.

But index funds are not immune to all silent partners, which is where inflation still is a factor. The best way to outpace inflation is to invest a large portion of a portfolio in stocks for as long as possible. Inflation has averaged 2.7 percent per year over the last five years, which amounts to a purchasing power loss of 27 percent to inflation over ten years.

So are Index Funds the Way to Go?

While the benefits are many, no investment in the financial world is without its disadvantages, and index funds are no different. The practice of investing in index funds comes with a lower yield than other investment opportunities, and some investors may consider this to be a disadvantage. Those who wish to be adventurous will want to try their hand at beating the stock market and living on the edge of financial ruin. For them, the relative security of the index fund is pointless, as they would not be satisfied with the average returns that are characteristic of index funds and instead prefer gambling on the stock market.

And while being adventurous is fun, it can be an especially dangerous game to play. The stock market can behave like a casino. Those who enter with an abundance of cash may come away with even bigger returns, but also keep in mind that the bigger the bet or investment, the bigger the loss.

The truth of the matter is that in the stock market world, you can throw a dart at a board and have the same luck as many of the investors who say they know an inside scoop.

The stock market moves so quickly and openly that whenever new information is revealed, the knowledge is instantly widespread, meaning that few have a greater advantage over anyone else.

All of these options come with higher risks and, by extension, higher rewards that lure the get-rich-quick crowd. Yet what many of them forget is that few becomes wealthy overnight, and if they do, it is by picking a few random, lucky numbers in the lottery.

Section 2

The concept of index funds, which took decades to materialize, has become a revolution, changing the stock market and showing investors that one is not required to beat the stock market to win.

In this next section we will leave behind the terminology, history, and advantages of the index fund and will begin looking at the variety of index funds available to investors.

In Chapter Four, we will examine equity index funds and the different investment opportunities, including choosing to follow a market capitalization index that invests in large-, mid-, small-, or micro-cap indexes. Choosing the market-cap that is best for individual needs helps understanding and management of portfolios better. Other types covered in this chapter include sector indexes, real estate investment trusts, and alternative types of indexes.

Chapter Five will focus on indexes that are not necessarily confined to companies in the United States, and Chapter Six will include other index funds that are less mainstream, such as commodity indexes and currency funds.

4

U.S. Equity Index Funds

"Everyone has the brainpower to follow the stock market. If you made it through fifth-grade math, you can do it."

- Peter Lynch, *Modern Maturity Magazine*, Jan./Feb. 1995

"I have probably purchased 50 'hot tips' in my career, maybe even more. When I put them all together, I know I am a net loser."

-Charles M. Schwab

Choosing an index fund is not as simple as it initially seems. A potential investor must look at the U.S. Equity Indexes before making a decision, which range from cap-weighted to sector-weighted.

As previously stated, an index is a compilation of various stocks on the market. The Dow Jones comprises 30 stocks from the U.S. Stock Market, while the S&P 500 has 500 stocks listed in its index. The greater the number of stocks held in an index, the less susceptible it is to fluctuations caused by large companies.

A U.S. Equity Index fund is categorized by the average size of the companies held in the index, resulting in four categories: large-cap, mid-cap, small-cap, and micro-cap.

Since the first market capitalization-weighted index was created by Standard and Poor's in 1923, the method of cap-weighted indexes has become the central principle of good equity index construction. Cap-weighting is the only weighting scheme consistent with a buy-and-hold strategy, allowing managers to keep pace with changes in the index constituents and reflecting modifications in index weights caused by changes in the number of shares outstanding in a constituent's company. Indexes based on market capitalization must be reconstituted occasionally to ensure they reflect the performance of the market segment they measure.

Market Capitalization

Market capitalization is the market price of an entire company, calculated by multiplying the number of shares outstanding by the price per share. Because owning a stock represents owning the company, capitalization represents the public opinion of a company's net worth, which is the determining factor in stock valuation. By March 2007, the market capitalization of every company in the world was $51.225 trillion.

If a company has a dominant shareholder, stock market indexes like the S&P 500, Sensex, FTSE, DAX, Nikkei, and MSCI will adjust by calculating a free-float basis, meaning that the market capitalization they use is the value of the publicly tradable part of the company. The market capitalization is based on perceived future prospects and economic and monetary conditions; therefore, a company's history does not have much of an effect on the dollar amount of the market capitalization.

Large-Cap Fund

If companies invest primarily in large company stocks with market values averaging more than $8 billion, they are classified as large-cap funds, which seek long-term growth potential and current income. Experts consider large-cap funds less volatile than funds invested in smaller companies, as they have a greater growth potential than bonds but also tend to be more volatile. Only 5 percent of all U.S. stocks are classified as large-cap, but that 5 percent comprises 80 percent of the wealth of the U.S. stock market. Examples of these stocks include General Electric, Microsoft Corporation, and ExxonMobil. There is no set criteria for what can be a large-cap and what cannot; one manager may consider a $4 billion company large-cap, while another would consider it mid-cap.

Mid-Cap Fund

When a company invests in smaller-sized company stocks with market values of $1 billion to $8 billion, they are deemed mid-cap funds. There is extra volatility with these types of caps because of investment in smaller companies, which creates volatility in the funds. Roughly 12 percent of all stocks are classified as mid-cap.

Small-Cap Fund

A fund that invests in companies with a market value below $1 billion is termed a small-cap fund. The volatility of these funds is dependent on managers; aggressive managers buy hot growth companies and take higher risks for higher rewards.

Other types of small-cap managers look for companies that have had trouble recently on the stock market, which are not as risky but are still quite volatile. Due to the risk related to small-cap funds, an investor needs time to compensate for short-term losses. Small-cap companies comprise the majority of the companies on the market — about 80 percent — but they only make up about 8 percent of the U.S. market value.

Micro-Cap Funds

Micro-cap funds invest in small companies with market values below $250 million. These managers look for startups, take-over candidate companies, or companies planning to find new markets. Investment in these funds comes at a high risk, but the growth potential can be immense. Bridgeway™ Ultra-Small Company is one example of a micro-cap company that, from 1995 to 1998, had an average annual growth rate of 15.9 percent. Only 2 percent of companies on the stock market are micro-cap, which do not trade with enough volume to make them appealing to a style manager looking for wide-scale mutual fund exploitation.

The Index Providers

There are several index providers in the U.S. equity market, thus it can be difficult to understand which to invest in. The major providers in the equity market are Frank Russell and Company, Standard and Poor's, MSCI, Morningstar®, and Dow Jones and Company.

Russell U.S. Equity Indexes

In 1936, Frank Russell started a small brokerage firm in Tacoma, Washington, which prospered in its small geographic location for more than two decades. George Russell joined his grandfather's firm in 1958 and became chairman, president, and CEO when his grandfather died. At this time, the Frank Russell Company comprised just two employees: George and an assistant. In 1969, George pioneered a new industry — strategic pension fund consulting — and, suddenly, things changed.

He presented his money manager evaluation process to JCPenney during a sales call and secured the company as his first client. He began managing money managers instead of the money and opened a New York office to expand across the country. By 1974, there would be 40 clients with Frank Russell and Company, including AT&T and General Motors. In 1979, Russell opened the first global office in London, and in 1980, they launched an investment management business in response to client requests for funds that provided a diversified index and packaged blend of investment managers. Four years later, in 1984, Russell and Company created the Russell 1000, Russell 2000, and Russell 3000 indexes as benchmarks to evaluate the performances of managers.

The company opened offices in Tokyo and Sydney during the following years, and in 1999, after being acquired by Northwestern Mutual, Russell, and Company appeared in *Fortune Magazine*'s "Best Companies to Work for in America" list, ranked at no. 15.

Years later, in 2007, Russell introduced a family of global indexes that captured 98 percent of the global equity market, reflecting the performance of more than 10,000 stocks worldwide and surpassing $4 trillion in benchmarked assets. The company now calculates 21 indexes daily, from the largest 200 growth companies to the small-cap value companies.

Every May 31st, Russell and Company ranks the top 3,000 largest U.S. stocks based on market capitalization. Any stock trading below $1 on that day is removed from the index, as well as closed-end mutual funds, limited partnerships, and royalty trusts.

Russell 3000 Index

This acts as the main index of the company, with the others acting as subsets. It measures the performance of the 3,000 largest companies in the United States based on their market capitalization, which makes up about 98 percent of the U.S. equity market.

The largest company on the index has a market capitalization of $410 billion, while the smallest has $95 million.

Russell 1000 Index

In the Russell 1000 Index, the 1,000 largest companies on the Russell 3000 Index are listed, or about 92 percent of its total market capitalization. The average market capitalization is $81 billion, and the smallest company on the index has a market capitalization of $1 billion.

Russell 2000 Index

In this sector, the index comprises 2,000 of the smallest companies on the Russell 3000 and just 8 percent of its total market capitalization. It has an average weighted market capitalization of $1 billion, with the largest company boasting a market capitalization of $2.4 billion, and the smallest a capitalization of $95 million.

Russell Top 50 Index

The 50 largest companies on the Russell 3000 Index are listed in the Russell Top 50 Index, which have an average market capitalization of $410 billion. The smallest company has $50 billion in market capitalization. This index makes up 41 percent of the total market value of the Russell 3000 Index.

Russell Mid-Cap Indexes

Only the 800 smallest companies on the Russell 1000 are listed on this index, which comprises 25 percent of the total market capitalization of the Russell 1000 Index. The average market capitalization is $7.5 billion.

Russell Micro-Cap Index

The smallest 1,000 securities on the small-cap Russell 2000 Index are in this index, making up less than 3 percent of the U.S. equity market. This index also includes the smallest 1,000 securities in the small-cap Russell 2000 Index, plus the next 1,000 securities, covering roughly 2,000 to 4,000 stocks.

Dow Jones Wilshire 5000 Composite Index

Founded in 1972 by Dennis Tito, a former scientist at the NASA Jet Propulsion Laboratory, Wilshire Associates is a leading provider of investment management, consulting, and technology services in Santa Monica, California. With a clientele valued at more than $12.5 trillion, it is a leading investment company thanks to the use of quantitative analytics, which uses mathematical tools to analyze market risks. Tito used these methods when determining a spacecraft's path at the Jet Propulsion Laboratory.

In the first decade of this century, Wilshire Associates teamed with Dow Jones and Company to give a broader spectrum of investment opportunities to investors. Notably, the Dow Jones Wilshire 5000 Composite Index became the first equity index in the United States to capture the entire return of the stock market.

While the Wilshire 5000 name implies there are 5,000 stocks on the index, the number of stocks on the index actually varies each week, rising above and below 5,000 due to mergers, buyouts, and bankruptcies. The Dow Jones Wilshire 5000 index uses two different measurements:

the full market capitalization measurement and the float-adjusted market capitalization measurement.

The full-market capitalization measurement takes the value of all the stocks outstanding, while the float-adjusted measurement does not include the value of privately held shares, restricted stock and shares held by other companies, and shares not available on the open market.

Stock additions and deletions from the index take place at the close of trading on the third Friday of every month. The index includes the companies that met inclusion criteria during the previous month.

Investors looking for the broadest range of stocks in the U.S. market will find it in an index fund, which is benchmarked to the Dow Jones Wilshire 5000. While investors may think they can benchmark their index fund against the entire index, it cannot be done due to the smaller stocks in the index not having enough liquidity or trade volume. In this case, the smaller stocks are infrequently bought by a large index fund.

To work around this, an index fund manager can sample the smaller stock universe by buying liquid small stocks representing industries and developing a portfolio that replicates the movement of the small-cap portion of the index without buying all the stocks in a selected group.

On average, a benchmark of the Dow Jones Wilshire 5000 is 3,000 stocks.

Dow Jones Wilshire 4500

Created on December 31, 1983, this index provider measures the performance of small- and mid-cap stocks on the Dow Jones Wilshire 5000.

The stock includes everything on the Dow Jones Wilshire 5000 index except the stocks listed on the S&P 500, which gives a benchmark for investors to see how non-S&P 500 stocks fare on the stock market.

Dow Jones Wilshire Micro-Cap Index

This index includes all the stocks on the Dow Jones Wilshire 5000 index below the 2,501 rank. The micro-cap index has about 2,600 stocks listed on it.

Morgan Stanley Capital International Indexes

In 1935, Henry S. Morgan and Harold Stanley founded Morgan Stanley, splitting commercial and investment banks to deal with the Glass-Steagall Act. Within a year, the company achieved a 24 percent market share, and by 1964, it created the first-ever computer model for financial analysis. The Morgan Stanley Group Inc. was listed publicly in 1986, and in 1996, it acquired Van Kampen American Capital, a respected mutual fund company.

The Morgan Stanley Capital International, formed in 1970, acquired Barra Inc. in 2004 to form MSCI Barra. Its headquarters are in New York, with additional offices in:

- Geneva
- London
- Mumbai
- Hong Kong
- Paris
- Tokyo
- Sao Paulo
- Sydney
- Frankfurt
- Milan
- Berkeley
- San Francisco

Morgan Stanley is the majority shareholder of MSCI Barra, while Capital Group Companies is the minority shareholder. Although the Morgan Stanley Capital International (MSCI) Index has only existed since 2002, it has created a broad index structure that reflects the investment opportunities across market capitalization size in the U.S. equity markets.

The MSCI uses all listed equity securities of U.S.-incorporated companies listed on the New York Stock Exchange, Amex, and NASDAQ. Not included in the MSCI indexes are incorporated companies outside the United States, investment trusts, mutual funds, equity derivatives, limited partnerships, limited liability, and business trusts.

The MSCI splits its indexes into large-cap, mid-cap, and small-cap. The large-cap index comprises 300 of the largest companies in the market segment; the mid-cap has the top 450 companies; and the small-cap lists the remaining 1,750 companies.

One unique aspect of the MSCI indexes is the use of buffer zones, which manage the migration of companies from one market capitalization to another. A company will enter the large-cap index when it reaches the market capitalization rank of 200, while a large-cap index company will leave when it drops to the rank of 451.

These buffer zones reduce trading losses by fund managers and others who attempt to beat changes to an index. They will often attempt to buy stocks added to indexes before managers can buy and sell stocks and before an index fund has time to sell.

MSCI Micro-Cap Index

All the securities in the top 99.5 percent of the U.S. equity universe that are not part of the 98 percent investable market index are included in the Micro-Cap Index. Also, all new companies and securities being considered for the Micro-Cap Index must have at least $20 million in full-market capitalization.

Morningstar® Indexes

This index was founded in 1984 by Joe Mansueto while he was the reviewing mutual fund annual reports he had requested from fund managers. After working as a stock analyst for Harris Associates and seeing the potential of the fund industry, he became convinced it could work. The company first operated out of his one-bedroom Chicago apartment, funded with an initial investment of $80,000. The name for the company was taken from the last sentence in *Walden* by Henry David Thoreau: "The sun is but a morning star."

In July 1999, Morningstar received an investment of $91 million from SoftBank in return for 20 percent of the company. On May 3, 2005, with 7,612,500 shares valued at $18.50 each, Morningstar went public. By following the pattern of Google, — using the Dutch auction method instead of the traditional method — it allowed investors to bid on the price of the stock, with all investors having equal access. As of March 2007, Mansueto owned 70 percent of the shares of Morningstar.

The Morningstar Indexes are composed of 15 size and style indexes that target about 97 percent of the free-float U.S. equity market. To be included in the indexes, companies must be domiciled in the United States, listed on the New York Stock Exchange and the Amex, and have historical, fundamental data available to classify its investment style. Not included are stocks that have more than ten non-trading days in the prior quarter.

The index is divided into large-cap, mid-cap, and small-cap, with the large cap making up 70 percent of the investable market cap, mid-cap making up 20 percent of the investable market cap, and small-cap making up 7 percent. Stocks are added or removed from the Morningstar indexes twice a year and rebalanced on a quarterly basis, though rebalancing does occur when a company's free-float changes by more than 10 percent or when two companies merge.

Morningstar also uses buffer zones to allow stocks to migrate between size and style categories over time. Short-term movements in buffer zones do not result in a high index turnover.

Standard and Poor's U.S. Equity Indexes

The Standard and Poor's indexes are considered the leaders in the financial world due to the amount of money benchmarked to the S&P 500 index, which is larger than all the other index funds combined. The selection criteria for Standard and Poor's indexes are very strict and, therefore, do not represent the entire stock market. Stocks are physically picked by a team of experts, a practice different than other indexes mentioned here. To be added to the index, a company must have a market capital in excess of $4 billion, financial viability, adequate liquidity, a public float of at least 50 percent, and must also operate in the United States.

Standard and Poor's indexes exclude stocks that trade at less than .3 percent of shares on average each month; are foreign issue or non-domicile U.S. stocks; and are closed-end funds or tracking stocks. Additionally, no single entity can own more than 50 percent of the stock in a company. An index can be removed if a company violates one or more of the criterion for inclusion or if a company is involved in a merger, acquisition, or reconstruction.

Standard and Poor's 500 Index

This index is used by 97 percent of money managers and pension plan sponsors, and the money that goes through this index is vast, amounting to more than $1 trillion invested by individuals and institutions. On average, the market value of the S&P 500 is $25 billion, primarily because it comprises large companies and has no real minimum limit on the size of a company to qualify for the index. The turnover average from 1926 to 2001 is 5 percent per year, with most companies exiting due to mergers and acquisitions. Within 30 days, a new company is selected by the Index Committee to fill the void of a company that has left the index.

Standard and Poor's 400 Mid-Cap Index

This index is used by mutual fund and pension plan sponsors to determine the performance of the mid-sized company segment of the U.S. financial market, with a total of $25 billion indexed to the 400 Mid-Cap Index. Companies on the index are split into two groups based on their price-to-book ratio, which creates growth and value indexes. The value index uses companies with a lower price-to-book ratio, while the growth index contains higher price-to-book ratios. Each index represents 50 percent of the market cap of the S&P 400.

Standard and Poor's Small-Cap Index

With $8 billion invested in this index, it is fast becoming the preferred benchmark for active and passive small-cap managers due to the low turnover on the index and the high liquidity. Like the 400 Mid-Cap Index, companies in this small-cap index are split into two groups based on price-to-book ratios to create growth and value indexes.

Standard and Poor's SuperComposite 1500 Index

This index is a combination of Standard and Poor's 500, Mid-Cap 400, and Small-Cap 600 indexes, and it comprises 85 percent of the total U.S. equity market capitalization.

Standard and Poor's 100 Index

This index measures the largest stocks in the United States, serving as a subset to the Standard and Poor's 500 Index. This is a free-float market capitalization-weighted index that has 100 major blue-chip stocks in it, representing 40 percent of the market value of all listed U.S. equities.

Standard and Poor's Market and Completion Index

This index represents the U.S. stock market, including listed equities on the New York Stock Exchange, Amex, NASDAQ National Market, and NASDAQ Small-Cap. The completion index is a subset of the total market index and includes all eligible stocks on the S&P Total Market Index but excludes constituents of the S&P 500, which allows it to cover 4,000 stocks. It offers a broad market exposure to mid-, small-, and micro-cap companies.

The NASDAQ

In 1971, the NASDAQ was created, becoming the world's first electronic stock market. It began as a computer bulletin board system but did not connect buyers and sellers. In turn, it helped lower the difference between the bidding and asking price of the stock, but it proved to be unpopular among brokerages because they made a great deal of their money off the spread. As time progressed, NASDAQ became more of a stock market by adding trade and volume reporting and trading systems. NASDAQ was also the first stock market to advertise to the common public. The main index for the company is the NASDAQ

Composite, which has been with it since its inception. The exchange-traded fund that tracks the large-cap NASDAQ 100 index was introduced in 1985, along with the NASDAQ 100 Financial Index.

In 1992, NASDAQ joined the London Stock Exchange to form the first intercontinental linkage of securities markets. By the first decade of the twenty-first century, it had become the largest electronic stock market in the United States.

In total, the NASDAQ lists 3,200 securities, 335 of which are non-U.S. companies from 35 countries in all industry sectors. To be part of the listing on the NASDAQ, a company must be registered with the SEC, have at least three market makers, and meet minimum requirements for assets, capital, public shares, and shareholders.

NASDAQ 100

This index includes 100 of the largest domestic and international non-financial securities listed on the NASDAQ market. It does not include securities of financial companies, including various investment companies.

Schwab 1000 Index and Fund

The Schwab 1000 Index Fund tracks the return of the Schwab 1000 index through the investment of the stocks of the 1,000 largest publicly traded U.S. Companies. This index is often compared with the Russell 1000 Index, and in April 2006, it celebrated its 15th year in a row with no capital gain distributions to shareholders.

Dow Jones U.S. Equity Averages and Indexes

As stated previously, the Dow Jones Industrial Average came into being in 1896 with a total of 12 stocks, which has now grown to 30. The Dow Jones and Company has created upwards of 3,000 U.S. and international market indexes, including those indexes that are based on industrial style.

Dow Jones U.S. Total Market Index

This index was launched in 2000 and represents 95 percent of the free-float value of the U.S. stock market, spanning a total of 1,850 stocks. Stocks on this index must have their headquarters and trading activity based in the United States. Stocks that are not included in this index are stocks that are traded infrequently or have low liquidity. Mutual funds, closed-end funds, limited partnerships, and Berkshire Hathaway Inc. also are excluded from this index.

Adjustments are made to indexes every quarter: March, June, September, and December. Public offerings are occasionally offered at the beginning of the quarter, and securities are removed from the index on the day they fail index inclusion guidelines. If a stock is removed from the index, it will not be replaced until the quarterly balancing is done.

Dow Jones Select Micro-Cap Index

This index measures the performance of micro-capitalization stocks traded on the U.S. stock exchanges. The index, which has more than 250 stocks, excludes stocks with low trading volumes to ensure that there are more investable stocks on the index.

Sector Index Funds

To allow mutual fund companies to create index funds benchmarked to industry classifications, index providers need to divide the stock market in terms of industry.

The concept of industry investing has become popular among investors because it allows funds to concentrate on a singular industry. This popularity comes with risks, like the bust of the tech bubble in the early 2000s, when technology stocks fell 80 percent between 2000 and 2002. A sector-fund investor will often have a portfolio that is spread through several sectors to ensure it is not susceptible to the rise and decline of one sector.

Classifying stocks by industries has become an efficient way to separate stocks on the various stock markets in the United States, allowing investors to understand the movement of capital from one industry to another.

Industry sectors may seem to be set in stone, but as new technology arises, new sectors arise. At the same time, other industries fade away to give the new sectors a place on the stock market and in investor portfolios.

Classifying Industry Sectors

Numbering on average between ten and 11, there are only a few industry sectors. The biggest difference between industry sectors is the subgroups that make up the classification. Each sector floats with the market, which can result in swings in industry value and cause the fortunes of some to quickly reverse. Clear examples of this are the changes that occurred in the industry leaders of the S&P between 1980 and 2000s.

In 1980, the largest industry sector was energy, which took up nearly one-quarter of the stocks on the S&P 500. Basic materials had 15 percent; consumer services had just over 5 percent; financials had 5 percent; and technology was at about 12 percent. By 2000, the energy sector was just over 6 percent with basic materials, and consumer services dropped a few percentage points as well. The financial sector shot up to just over 15 percent, while the technology sector nearly doubled to just under 30 percent.

Evidently, an industry's value on the stock market can rapidly change. That being said, the technology sector quickly fell during the first decade of the twenty-first century, while the energy sector percentage began to increase.

The Global Industry Classification Standard

Two of the leading global index providers, Standard and Poor's and Morgan Stanley Capital International, created the Global Industry Classification Standard (GICS) in 1999. The global financial community needed a complete set of global sector and industry definitions that could reflect the economy but would be flexible enough to change as the investment world changed, and this standard offered a solution. Since 1999, more than 34,000 companies in the world have been classified and maintained according to GICS methodology.

The structure of the GICS is split into four levels: sector, industry group, industry, and sub-industry. Currently, there are ten sectors, 24 industry groups, 67 industries, and 147 sub-industries. Each spring, changes that range from the renaming of industries to the addition of sub-industries are made to the GICS.

The ten sectors that make up the GICS are:

1. Basic materials
2. Consumer discretionary
3. Consumer stables
4. Energy
5. Financial
6. Health care
7. Industrials
8. Information Technology
9. Telecommunication services
10. Utilities

Industry Classification Benchmark

The Dow Jones and the FTSE have helped create a classification system called the Industry Classification Benchmark, which contains more than 40,000 companies and 45,000 securities worldwide. This benchmark offers global coverage of companies and securities by classifying them based on revenue, not earnings.

The Industry Classification Benchmark and the GICS are similar with the exception of some sub-sectors that fall under different categories between the two classification systems. The structure of the Industry Classification Benchmark is ten industries, 18 super-sectors, 39 sectors, and 104 sub-sectors. The names of the sectors in the Industry Classification Benchmark are the same as those in the GICS.

Merrill Lynch HOLDRS

Charles E. Merrill opened for business at 7 Wall Street in New York City in 1914. He was joined a few months later by his friend Edmund C. Lynch, effectively changing their name to Merrill Lynch in 1915. Over the decades, Merrill Lynch rose to prominence through the strength of its brokerage network, which numbered to more than 15,000 in 2006. This huge network led them to be referred to as a thundering herd because they were able to place the securities they underwrote directly. This is in sharp contrast to other firms that relied on selling groups of independent brokers for placement of the securities they underwrote.

In 1971, the firm went public and has since become a multinational corporation, with $1.8 trillion in client assets.

Merrill Lynch introduced unit investment trusts, called HOLDRS, in 2000. These securities are exchange-traded funds that have similar characteristics to other exchange-traded funds. HOLDRS are unique because they invest in the top 20 stocks of industry sectors and sub-sectors using the GICS, yet they are not a true index fund because they do not attempt to replicate a particular industry group. HOLDRS invest the same amount of money in each stock of an industry sector.

Investors can turn in HOLDRS in rounds of 100 units and receive the underlying stock in return, which allow an investor to sell specific stocks in a fund, rather than the entire fund. HOLDRS are termed a non-managed unit investment trust that results in no management fee, although there is an annual charge of $2 per 100-unit trustee and custody fee that is paid to the Bank of New York from stock dividends.

Real Estate Investment Trust Index Funds

Real estate is treated as a different asset class than stocks because tax accounting is different than stocks for real estate, as are collaterals of Real Estate Investment Trusts (REIT).

Previously one could only invest in real estate through direct ownership or limited partnerships. Now, investors can buy an assortment of real estate through a computer by buying a REIT on the stock exchange.

This is an untapped asset class with a market valued somewhere around $5 trillion. It represents 5.2 percent of the U.S. gross domestic product (GDP), yet only 5 percent of the institutional portfolios are held in real estate assets.

Real estate also can act as a hedge against inflation because property values have historically kept pace with universal price inflation, especially during periods of inflation pressure. Also, some commercial leases are indexed to the current inflation rate, which lock real returns during periods of inflation.

A REIT represents an investment in a group of real properties, with the investor buying a management company that acquires and manages commercial real estate. The company collects rent on the properties and distributes those rents to the shareholders.

This type of trust is similar to closed-end mutual funds because they trade at a premium or a discount on the value of the assets. Because the value of a property can only be known when it is sold, the market value of REITs fluctuates with supply and demand. REITs have positive tax benefits as well, including management companies that are not required to pay corporate tax on any distributions to shareholders, as long as 90 percent of the income is passed to the shareholders. At least three-quarters of the income in the company must be from rents, mortgages, and the sales of real estate properties. As a result, the dividend income from REIT Index Funds is far higher than any other equity index fund.

Adding these types of index funds to a portfolio lowers risk and increases return because of the low correlation in return between REITs, stocks, and bonds.

Investing in Real Estate Investment Trusts

REITs address the shortcomings of private equity real estate investments by offering liquidity, diversification, and professional management. They allow for an investment in the right property with the right people at the right price, all in one investment.

Even though REITs have benefits over private equity vehicles, they make up only 10 percent of the U.S. investment-grade real estate market.

REITs have a focused investment strategy, concentrating resources on one property type or geographic area, which brings expertise in the acquisition and management of particular types of real estate portfolios.

Between 1975 and 1999, REITs provided a rate of return of 16 percent, compared to the 17.2 percent of the S&P 500 Index, showing that REITs can outperform certain indexes on the market.

Morgan Stanley U.S. Real Estate Investment Trust

This index was designed as a representation of REITs, representing 85 percent of the REITs in the United States. The index comprises REITs included in the MSCI US Investable Market 2500 Index. Any equity REITs that do not generate a majority of their income from real estate rental and leasing are not included in this index, nor are any mortgages or hybrid REITs or companies under the GICS Real Estate Management and Development sub-industry.

In total, this index has 112 companies on it.

Dow Jones U.S. Real Estate Index

This index of about 93 companies makes up the real estate portion of the Dow Jones U.S. Total Market Index. The Dow Jones U.S. Real Estate Index has REITs but also includes real-estate operating companies listed on it. A subset of this index is the Dow Jones Wilshire REIT Index, which includes only REITs holding 85 components.

S&P REIT Composite Index

This index tracks 100 REITs in the U.S. markets, all of which are chosen for their liquidity and importance in terms of representing a diversified portfolio. For an REIT to be included in this, they must have $100 million in unadjusted market capitalization and meet the same liquidity guidelines of the S&P Super-Composite 1500.

Cohen & Steers Realty Majors Index

The performance of large and actively traded U.S. real estate investment trusts are tracked on this index. This index holds only 30 REITs and has no major mortgage lenders.

Indexes for the Socially-Responsible

There are investors who face dilemmas related to how businesses in the index fund make a profit. As a result, some indexes reject companies that do not pass a social criteria test. Exclusions may include companies that sell tobacco and alcohol products or deal in pornography. Companies known for violations of labor practices and human and animal rights may also be excluded. Visit **www.socialinvest.org** to find a socially responsible index fund.

FTSE4Good U.S. Select Index

This index is made and maintained by the FTSE Group, which selects stocks from 700 of the largest public companies in the United States. Each company is evaluated on the basis of including environmental sustainability and supporting human rights. Companies based in the tobacco, alcohol, pornography, firearms, gambling, and nuclear power industries are excluded from this index.

KLD Broad Market Social Index

This index uses the Russell 3000 Index and removes any company in the pornography, alcohol, firearms, gambling, military, nuclear power, and tobacco industries. Each company is ranked in the index in terms of community and corporate governance, diversity, employee relations, product quality, and human rights. KLD also runs the KLD Select Social Index, which is less restrictive than the Broad Market Social Index and only excludes tobacco stocks.

Domini 400 Social Index

This index uses the S&P 500 and removes any company in the alcohol, tobacco, firearms, gambling, nuclear power, and military industries. Only companies with a positive social and environmental record are selected for this index.

Calvert Social Index

This index uses 1,000 of the largest companies in the United States and eliminates all of those in the alcohol, tobacco, gambling, nuclear power, and animal testing industries. Currently, there is no low-cost index fund benchmarked to the Calvert Social Index.

Alternative U.S. Equity Funds

There are several index funds that make minor changes from an index to enhance returns to investors that will do little harm to an investor's portfolio in case of failed strategies. This is in contrast to funds that are completely out of the real world of the index fund, often called "radical funds," which can drain your portfolio if the market takes a turn for the worse.

There are several types of special funds, including enhanced, leveraged, inverse index, modified-weight, and equal-weight.

As a rule, index funds are capitalization-weighted, with stocks selected for an index on the grounds of their market capitalization. These stocks take precedence in an index according to their market value.

Any weighting attempt other than a market-cap method is considered to be a modified stock-weighting scheme. These methods of modification include fundamental, factor, and equal weights. Fundamental weighting is based on the ranking of sales, cash flow, and dividends. Factor weighting is similar to fundamental weighting, but it is based on financial ratios only. Equal weighting allocates the same amount of capital to each stock in an index.

Portfolios that have the same stocks as an index, with the weights of the stocks manipulated, are no longer considered to be following an index. If this is the case, it is simply a portfolio of stocks, not an index fund.

Supporters of modified stock-weight methods say that cap-weighted indexes are inefficient and that changing the weight of the stocks creates a better index.

This is considered to be untrue by many in the financial community. When managers claim that changing the weight makes a better index, they are wrong; changing the weight of stocks results in a portfolio that no longer follows the index.

Equal-Weight Funds

Equal-weight funds are the easiest to modify and to understand. Mutual fund companies will start with all the stocks in a cap-weighted index before giving each stock an equal weight in the portfolio. This practice thins the allocation to large stocks and places significantly more capital in mid- and small-cap stocks in an index.

What is a Dividend?

Dividends are payments made by a company to its shareholders. When a company earns a profit, the money can be re-invested in the business or can be paid to the shareholders in the form of a dividend.

Dividends may seem like an expense but are actually divisions of assets among shareholders. Publicly traded companies frequently pay dividends on a fixed schedule, but this is not set in stone. A "special" dividend can be paid at any time.

Dividends are frequently settled as a cash-basis payment from the company to the shareholder. Dividends can take the form of shares in the company, and many companies offer dividend reinvestment plans, which automatically use the cash dividend to purchase more shares for the shareholder.

In the United States, dividends are most often paid quarterly by the board of directors. In some countries, dividends are paid biannually as an interim dividend shortly after the company announces its interim results, and as a final dividend following an annual meeting.

This all deals with a company making a profit. If a company has a loss for the year, it can decide to pay dividends through retained earnings from previous years or choose to discontinue the dividend.

When there is a non-recurring gain through the sale of assets, a special dividend is issued to shareholders. This dividend is often larger than usual dividends and occurs outside the regular dividend schedule. The dividend can come in several forms: cash, stock, and property, among others. The cash dividend, which is the most common, is paid in the form of a check. This type of dividend is a form of investment income and is taxable to the shareholder.

Stock is paid to some shareholders as a form of dividend, often issued in the proportion of shares owned. In other words, for every 100 shares of stock a shareholder owns, he or she will receive an extra five shares on a 5 percent stock dividend. This is called a stock split because it increases the number of shares while lowering the price of each share without changing market capitalization or the total value of the held shares. Property can be given as dividends that are identified as dividends in specie, which are paid in the form of assets from the corporation or through a subsidiary corporation. It is rare for this type of dividend to be paid. Dividends can be used in other forms such as structured finance, in which assets have a known market value that can be distributed as dividends.

The declaration date of a dividend is the day that the board of directors announces the decision to pay them out. When this is done, a liability is created and recorded in the company's books, stating that it now owes the money to shareholders. Another significant date is the ex-dividend date, which is the day after all shares are bought, sold, and no longer attached with the right to be paid the most recently declared dividend. This date is important because it makes reconciliation of who is to be paid the dividend easier.

Before this date, the stock is said to be "with dividend." Existing shareholders and anyone who buys it will receive the dividend, whereas sellers will lose their right to the dividend. On or after this date, the stock is an ex-dividend, and existing holders of the stock will still receive the dividend even if they sell their stock at that point. Those who buy the stock after that date will not receive the dividend.

Other noteworthy dates for a dividend are the record date, during which a shareholder properly registers their ownership, and the payment date, when dividends are paid out.

There are several benefits to shareholders in terms of dividends. Shareholders have their own personal cash flow and needs, and they self-reflect the companies whose dividends satisfy these. Also, common share dividends are popular with preferred shareholders because they create a cushion that must be cut before their own dividends are. Furthermore, shareholders feel that the risk of returns from reinvested earnings at a later date is higher than the risk of cash received today. Finally, the retaining of earnings affects how management dictates to owners how to invest their money.

Dividend-Weighted Funds

After the collapse of the tech stock market in the early 2000s, investors turned to dividend-paying stocks and mutual funds because most tech companies did not pay dividends. Their reasoning was that the companies that paid dividends were more stable than those that did not. Essentially, dividend funds are based on dividend indexes that differ from market-weighted indexes in two ways: They are screened for constant dividend payments over a period of time, and the stocks in the index are weighted according to the yield of a dividend rather than market capitalization.

We know that an index regularly measures a stock index made up of a certain sector or criteria, whereas dividend indexes measure nothing and cannot be used as a benchmark for a market or for comparing active managers. They are only useful for licensing to a mutual fund company that will then create a mutual fund.

Dividend-weighted funds are considered to be value stocks because the companies that pay dividends are normally at a point of mature development. Typically, a company that pays dividend growth has an earning growth and price-to-earning ratio that is lower, while the book value and cash flow is higher. While technology, communications, and media stocks offer little exposure to dividend indexes, financial, energy, health care, and industrial stocks do.

Dow Jones Dividend Index

This index mirrors the performance of 100 leading U.S. dividend-paying companies. In this index, stocks are selected based on their dividend yield, and index constituents are dividend-weighted rather than market capitalization-weighted. The dividend weight is determined by the size and strength of the dividend. Of all the dividend indexes, the Dow Jones Dividend Index is the most diverse.

S&P High Yield Dividend Aristocrat Index

Designed to reflect the performance of the 50 highest dividend-yielding stocks in the S&P SuperComposite 1500, this index requires that a company must have consistent annual increases for at least 25 consecutive years. While other dividend indexes specialize in one or two sectors, this index spreads itself across many different sectors.

Morningstar Dividend Leaders Index

This index uses the 100 highest-yielding stocks, which have consistent records of dividend payment, and weights them in proportion to the total pool of dividends available to investors. The dividend that a company pays must be equal or greater to the dividend paid five years ago for inclusion on this index.

The Dividend Achievers Select Index

If a stock has a record of increasing dividends for at least ten years in a row, it can be included in this index. REITs and companies with low dividend growth are not included. Vanguard by Mergent, Inc. administers this index using a yield-driven weighting methodology rather than a market-cap one and is one of the most diverse dividend indexes.

Fundamental Weighting

With fundamental weighting, stocks are still selected from a cap-weighted benchmark, but the weights of the portfolio will shift if a company's fundamentals shift as well, rather than the price of the stock.

FTSE Research Affiliates Fundamental Index U.S. 1000

This index uses the fundamental-weighting process by calculating the percentage representation of each stock using sales, cash-flow, book value, and dividends. The stocks are then ranked in descending order based on their Research Affiliates Fundamental Index (RAFI) score, with the largest 1,000 U.S. companies designated as index constituents.

So many indexes...

The number of indexes may be overwhelming, but these indexes are only the market-capitalization and sector-based indexes; other types of indexes are still available, including international and commodity indexes.

The indexes outlined in this past chapter are by no means all of the ones available to you, but they are the best ones for an investor to investigate. They are driven by established companies that have pioneered the concept of indexes and index funds. As a result, service is of the highest quality with these indexes.

Looking at your own finances and your experience as an investor, decide what kind of index you want to choose for your portfolio. With so many choices, including large-, mid-, small-, and micro-cap, an investor must analyze every detail before making a decision.

RICH
Senior Vice

5

Global & International Equity

"A market is the combined behavior of thousands of people responding to information, misinformation, and whim."

-Kenneth Chang

"Emotions are your worst enemy in the stock market."

-Don Hays

In a trend that few could have predicted, the global equity market grew quickly over the past half-century. In the 1970s, international stock markets were 30 percent of the global equity market, with the American stock accounting for 70 percent. But times have changed, and now the American stock market accounts for less than 50 percent of the global equity market — a dramatic change of events for global equity. In 1970, Europe comprised 22 percent of the global market share, while Asia and other countries accounted for 7 and 3 percent. By October 2006, Europe was 32 percent, Asia 17 percent, and other countries were 2 percent.

While the international equity markets have grown in number, size, and scope, the number of index funds benchmarked to international markets also has rapidly increased.

During the recession between 2001 and 2003, global merger and acquisition activities were hampered because a surge in mergers and acquisitions across the world in the late 1990s and early 2000s blurred the distinction between domestic and foreign companies with stocks.

Attaining international exposure in a portfolio of stock index funds will lower the risk and increase portfolio returns due to the diversity of the portfolio. International stocks are valued in native currency, which protect an investor against devaluation of the American dollar.

Major index investors have been in competition for dominance in global equity benchmarks for more than a decade, and it was not until the late 1990s that the four leading international index providers — MSCI, FTSE, S&P, and Dow Jones — began to heat things up.

Understanding International Investing

International indexes comprise stocks from corporations that have main headquarters outside the United States. International indexes are also called foreign or overseas indexes.

World or global indexes invest in both U.S. and international stocks. There also are regional indexes that invest in stocks outside a specific geographical area, such as Latin America or the Pacific Rim. Regional indexes also invest in a region minus a certain country. For example, a regional index may be for Latin America minus Brazil.

Two types of market indexes are based on a country's current development: Developed market indexes comprise countries whose governments and economies are advanced and have a per capita GDP of at least $10,000. Examples of developed markets include most of Europe, Australia, Japan, and Canada. Emerging market indexes consist of countries that are less advanced, with a lower per capita GDP and a primitive free-market system. This type of market can be divided into two types: early-stage and late-stage. An example of early-stage emerging markets are Turkey, Poland, Indonesia, and Russia, while the advanced late-stage emerging markets include Mexico, South Korea, and India.

Developed Market Indexes and Funds

There are 23 developed markets in which investments may be made.

1. Australia
2. Austria
3. Belgium
4. Canada
5. Denmark
6. Finland

7. France
8. Germany
9. Greece
10. Hong Kong
11. Ireland
12. Italy
13. Japan
14. Netherlands
15. New Zealand
16. Norway
17. Portugal
18. Singapore
19. Spain
20. Sweden
21. Switzerland
22. United Kingdom
23. United States

The Morgan Stanley Capital International Europe, Australasia, and the Far East Index (MSCI EAFE) is the most widely quoted index, and is the benchmark by which most developed country index funds are compared against. The MSCI EAFE index comprises 1,000 company stocks from 21 developed countries in Europe and the Pacific Rim, which includes 85 percent of the free-float market value of each country's industry groups.

It essentially covers all developed countries except the United States and Canada. Because this index does not try to control sector weights, it is susceptible to dramatic swings between industry sectors, countries, and regions. A good example of this is Japan, which dominated the index in 1990 with 70 percent of the weight. Due to a slow market in Japan and a powerful European market in recent years, it now represents only 2 percent of the index. The index is divided into growth and value styles, with an objective to divide constituents of an underlying MSCI standard country index into a value or growth index.

The FTSE International Limited Developed ex-North America Index has about 1,300 stocks from 20 countries around the world, including Japan, the United Kingdom, and developed countries in Continental Europe and the Pacific Rim.

Charles Schwab also has its own developed markets index, called the Schwab Total International Index, which includes stock from 15 developed countries outside the United States. In these countries, Schwab has identified the 350 largest companies in terms of market capitalization, with no country taking up more than 35 percent of the index.

The Vanguard Developed Market Fund is weighted to the Vanguard Pacific Stock Index Fund and the Vanguard European Stock Index Fund. Vanguard also developed the Total International Portfolio, which consists of the Vanguard Pacific Stock Index Fund, the Vanguard European Stock Index Fund, and the Vanguard Emerging Stock Index Fund.

Dimensional Fund Advisors (DFA) has managed capitalization equities in international markets since 1986, when regional portfolios were created in the United Kingdom and Japan. For the past 20 years, DFA has added company portfolios in Europe and the Pacific Rim and now offers a small capitalization stocks in all four regions. DFA trades small company stocks through its London and Sydney offices and also offers large and small company portfolios, designed to capture the value effect that is defined by individual countries.

Emerging Market Indexes and Funds

The term "emerging market" became popular in the 1980s when World Bank economist Antoine van Agtmael used the phrase to describe the economies of countries that were termed "third-world," as the phrase "third-world economy" sparked images of starving people, and the decision was made to find a different name.

The label was based on emerging economies, but it also signified a business phenomenon that was not fully limited to geography or economic strength. Ian Bremmer, a political scientist, defined an emerging market as a country where politics matter at least as much to the markets as economics.

The term has existed for almost 30 years, but there is still no consensus on what an emerging market really is. The concept is not well-understood in spite of substantial research and literature written from C.K. Prahalad, George Haley, Hernando De Sota, Usha Haley, Rajesh K. Pillania, and professors from Harvard and Yale.

Several types of emerging markets exist, including those in an intersection of non-traditional user behavior, such as the rise of new user groups and community adoption of products and services through the innovations in product technologies.

Another form of emerging markets are the rapidly developing and growing economies of the United Arab Emirates, Chile, and Malaysia. For the best guides in defining an emerging market, explore sources like ISI Emerging Markets, The Economist, or Morgan Stanley Capital International, which are all well-informed publications

However, two problems emerge due to the nature of the investment information sources. The first is the element of historicity, which means markets may continue in an index for continuity, even if the countries have developed past the emerging market phase. Examples of these types of countries include South Korea, Taiwan, Singapore, Israel, and the Czech Republic.

The second problem is the simplification that is inherent in an index. The small countries have a limited market liquidity that is not considered, so their larger, neighboring countries are used as stand-ins for them on the index.

As of July 2006, emerging markets on the Morgan Stanley Emerging Markets Index included:

1. Argentina
2. Brazil
3. Chile
4. China
5. Colombia
6. Czech Republic
7. Egypt
8. Hungary
9. India
10. Indonesia

11. Israel
12. Jordan
13. Malaysia
14. Morocco
15. Pakistan
16. Peru
17. Philippines
18. Poland
19. Russia
20. Slovakia
21. South Africa
22. South Korea
23. Taiwan
24. Thailand
25. Turkey

This is a partial list, though, and does not include every country.

According to the *Grant Thornton International Business Report*, published on April 19, 2007, there are four emerging markets that investors should keep an eye on: Mexico, Indonesia, Pakistan, and Turkey. These countries have been identified as the next generation of emerging markets that will have a significant impact on the worldwide economy.

Mexico has already been identified as an important economy in the BRIMC (Brazil, Russia, India, Mexico, and China) and the G8+5. Theorists have postulated that these countries could match or overtake the BRIC countries

(Brazil, Russia, India, and China), which are expected to join the global economic powers. That being said, these countries are unlikely to match the economic growth of India or China. Indonesia and Pakistan have especially large populations and, as a result, have great potential for labor intensive exports that could capitalize on the process of low-cost production.

BRIMC

An anagram of Brazil, Russia, India, Mexico, and China, the term was created by the Goldman Sachs investment bank thesis titled "BRIC." When the paper was written in 2001, Jim O'Neill, an expert from the same bank, said that they did not initially consider Mexico. But today, Mexico is experiencing the same type of growth as the countries that were first presented.

The paper stated that the BRIMCs are rapidly developing, and by 2050, they will eclipse most of the rich countries in the world. The term has seen its usage grow in the investment sector and is now being used to refer to bonds emitted by these emerging markets.

The S&P Emerging Market Indexes have existed since 1975, growing to more than 2,000 companies in 53 markets around the world. These indexes are divided into two main groups: The S&P/IFCG Indexes are broad market indicators that measure the opportunity set of investable stocks in each emerging market, and the S&P IFCI (Investable) indexes are subsets of the IFCG indexes.

The S&P labels a country "emerging" if it has a low- or middle-income economy and the country's investable market capitalization is low in terms of its GDP figures. So far, the database of emerging markets is nearing 60.

The S&P/IFCG targets a market capitalization of about 70 to 80 percent of all the capitalization of all exchange-listed shares. To be on the index, a company has to be domiciled in an emerging market and be among the most actively traded securities in that market. To be included in the S&P/IFCI, the company must have a minimum average investable market capitalization of $125 million and trade at least $50 million in the 12 months prior to addition.

The MSCI Emerging Markets Index is a free-float adjusted market capitalization index that measures equity market performance for emerging markets. MSCI designates a market as emerging based on per capita GDP government regulations, investment risk, foreign ownership limits, and capital controls. This market comprises 25 emerging market country indexes in:

1. Argentina
2. Brazil
3. Chile
4. China
5. Colombia
6. Czech Republic
7. Egypt
8. Hungary
9. India
10. Indonesia
11. Israel
12. Jordan
13. Korea
14. Malaysia
15. Mexico
16. Morocco
17. Pakistan
18. Peru
19. Philippines
20. Poland
21. Russia
22. South Africa
23. Taiwan
24. Thailand
25. Turkey

Regional Index Funds

The EAFE is split into two large geographic regions by the MSCI, forming the MSCI Europe Index and the MSCI Pacific Index. The process of dividing indexes into regions allows index funds to be benchmarked to specific regions.

The MSCI Europe Index consists of nearly 600 stocks in companies located in 16 European countries, including:

1. United Kingdom
2. France
3. Switzerland
4. Germany
5. Austria
6. Belgium
7. Denmark
8. Finland
9. Greece
10. Ireland
11. Italy
12. Netherlands
13. Norway
14. Portugal
15. Spain
16. Sweden

The MSCI Pacific Index comprises 546 common stocks of companies in Japan, Australia, Hong Kong, Singapore, and New Zealand. Japan makes up 75 percent of the index's market capitalization, while Australia makes up 16 percent.

The S&P Global 1200 index is divided into various regional indexes, including the S&P Europe 350 Index, which measures the performance of all the stocks in continental Europe and the United Kingdom. The stocks on this index are chosen for market size, liquidity, industry group representation, and geographic diversity.

As a result of the Euro and the move for a common currency across the European continent, there has been a greater opportunity to create indexes in that region.

The MSCI United Kingdom Index benchmarks publicly traded securities in the aggregate in the British markets. Currently, the United Kingdom, Sweden, and Denmark are the only developed countries in Europe that are not in the Eurozone — that is, countries that use the Euro.

The Dow Jones STOXX 50 Index provides blue-chip representation of Supersector leaders in Europe. The index includes companies in Austria, Belgium, Denmark, Finland, France, Germany, Portugal, Spain, Sweden, Switzerland, and the United Kingdom.

The S&P Latin America 40 includes highly liquid securities from major sectors of Mexico, Brazil, Argentina, and Chile, with companies representing 70 percent of each country's market cap.

Global Market Indexes and Funds

One smart strategy when buying one stock index fund is to consider a global-developed market fund. The three main worldwide providers of these types of funds are Standard and Poor's, Dow Jones, and Morgan Stanley Capital Investments (MSCI). S&P and MSCI often work together to compile data and contrast indexes.

Morgan Stanley Capital Investments Global Indexes

This index combines the MSCI All Country World Index and the MSCI Global Total Bond Index to span global stock and bond markets. The market capitalization of the MSCI Global Index is almost $30 trillion in equity and more than

$20 trillion in fixed income. U.S. equities make up just under 30 percent of the index, and U.S. bonds make up just under 20 percent. There are now more than 11,500 securities in the MSCI Global Capital Markets Index.

The MSCI All Country World Index is a free-float adjusted market capitalization equity index that measures market performance of the developed and emerging markets around the world. The MSCI All Country World Index currently includes 50 countries and has an inclusion rate of 85 percent of free-float adjusted market capitalization in every industry group in each country. There are currently no index funds benchmarked to the MSCI All Country World Index.

The S&P Global Indexes

One index that combines the features of a broad global portfolio with excellent liquidity in the underlying equities is the S&P Global 1200 Index, which is suited for index-related investment products. It is a free-float weighted index constructed with Morgan Stanley although, presently, there are no index funds benchmarked to it. In total, it covers 70 percent of the global capitalization market and is composed of the S&P 500, S&P Europe 350, S&P/TOPIX 150 (Japan), S&P/TSX 60 (Canada), S&P Asia Pacific 100, and S&P Latin America 40. A committee of Standard & Poor's staff selects companies for inclusion into the index.

The S&P Global 100 comprises the 100 leading companies listed in the S&P Global 1200, which attains most of its income through multiple countries. This does not mean that those 100 countries are the largest, however; the rankings are based on industry leadership, market liquidity, and size. Almost half of the companies in the index are from the United States, with Europe taking up 30 percent of the index. The largest holding in the index is ExxonMobil, which has 5 percent of the index.

Dow Jones Global Titans 50 Index

In spite of creating the concept of the index over 100 years ago, Dow Jones is not considered to be a leader in global index construction — but they are making headway.

The only noteworthy global index offered by Dow Jones is the Dow Jones Global Titans 50, which is made of the 50 largest companies in the world. But a company must be well-established with a solid financial and client base, well-known to investors for success, and a market leader in its industry.

On average, Dow Jones will screen 5,000 stocks for size and liquidity to create a pool of 100 countries, with each company in the pool deriving some of its income from foreign operations. The stocks are then ranked based on asset size, book value, sales, and net profit, then divided into industry groups and sorted by market value.

Country Index Funds

Many different country index funds are benchmarked to the MSCI country indexes, which constructs an index for each country by listing every security on the market and collecting price data, outstanding shares, significant ownership, and free-float and monthly trading volumes. Stocks are categorized by industry, with the MSCI methodology requiring 8 percent of the market capitalization of that country. Industry replication is a key characteristic of a single-country market index.

A World of Indexes

It should be no surprise that a concept that was created in Denmark hundreds of years ago has spread across the world to put a stock market in almost every country around the world. When we are talking about the world of finance, we too often focus on the United States without considering the other markets that exist in the world. No market is the same as another and, depending on the countries' situations, the market may be more primitive than others.

To help understand the markets of the world, without excluding any, economic theorists have developed several terms for the markets. Most of the items related to finance, the wealth of the world, and those who invest are in developed countries. Consequently, these are the world leaders in many areas and are often considered to be the dominant countries on Earth.

On the other hand, emerging countries are those that are making headway but are not quite there. Countries like China, Russia, and India still have other factors — not related to finance — that they need to improve upon, including human rights. Many of these countries are advancing quickly, though, and may eventually overtake the largest markets in the world, perhaps by mid-century.

In a reversal of financial fortunes, today's emerging markets will be tomorrow's dominant, developed markets.

Investing in country, regional, and global indexes is a risky venture. But with risk comes rewards, including not suffering as much from the issues of your native country's stock market. By investing in other country indexes in companies that are based elsewhere, one can benefit from new innovations and acquisitions that may occur elsewhere in the world.

This is doubly true for emerging markets in the world. By recognizing who is going to rise and who is going to fall on the global scale, an investor can benefit from getting involved with companies that are likely to change the future of the world. Investors may not benefit immediately, but China, Russia, Mexico, India, and Brazil are catching up fast, and the benefits in the future could be immense.

6

Commodity & Currency Funds

"The ability to deal with people is as purchasable a commodity as sugar or coffee, and I will pay more for that ability than for any other under the sun."

-John D. Rockefeller

Over the past few years, index funds have expanded beyond stock and bond funds and are now available in several alternative classes, including commodities, commodity indexes, and currencies.

One great advantage in adding an alternative asset class such as commodities to a portfolio is that individual commodity sectors tend to have a low correlation with each other, creating lower portfolio risk, which could increase long-term return.

However, disadvantages include the cost of investing in commodities, which is higher than stock and bond index funds, and the lack of expected return over fees, inflation, and low tax-efficiency.

What Are Commodities?

The word "commodity" first came into use in the fifteenth century, coming from the French word "commodite," which translates as "convenience. "

Commodities are common products like food, basic materials, and energy-related items that individuals use daily. Primarily, there are six categories of commodities:

- Energy: oil, gas, and electricity
- Industrials: copper, steel, and cotton
- Precious Metals: gold, platinum, silver, and aluminum
- Livestock: cattle and hogs
- Grains and Oilseeds: corn, soybeans, and wheat
- Softs: cocoa, coffee, orange juice, and sugar.

Since these are items that people use every day, the global market for commodities is expansive. Almost every nation of the world has commodities that are excavated, manufactured, or grown, creating hundreds of commodity markets.

Commodities come in an abundance to every country, yet there are many more to be grown, manufactured, and excavated. While shortages in these sectors can exist, they are marginalized over time. If a commodity such as wheat rises in price because of greater demand, farmers will grow more wheat the next season and continue to do so until supply exceeds demand and the price begins to fall.

A commodity is also defined as "anything that is in demand." Commodity prices are, by and large, determined as a function of their market as a whole, with well-established physical commodities having actively traded spots and derivative markets.

Commoditization occurs as goods or services lose their differentiation across a supply base. Often, it is caused by the diffusion of intellectual capital that is necessary to produce it efficiently. As a result, goods that carried premium margins for market participants have become commodities, including pharmaceuticals and silicon chips.

Commodity Trade

Commodities are items of value in uniform quantities, produced in large numbers by various companies. It is the contract and this standard that define the commodity, not any quality inherent in the product. Somc commodity exchanges include the Chicago Board of Trade, Euronext. liffe, London Metal Exchange, New York Mercantile Exchange, and the Multi Commodity Exchange.

Markets used for trading commodities can be rather efficient, especially when there is a division into pools matching segments. These markets have the ability to quickly respond to changes in supply and demand to find the price that will reach equilibrium. Investors can also gain passive exposure to commodity markets through a commodity price index.

Another Type of Index?

A commodity price index is simply a fixed-weight index of commodity prices, designed to be a representation of the broad commodity asset class, or certain subsets like energy and metals. By choice, investors will often obtain a passive exposure to these price indexes through a total return swap. The advantages of this include a negative correlation with other asset classes. Disadvantages include a negative roll yield due, which can be reduced by active management techniques such as reducing the weight of constituents in the index.

Futures

Included in lists of commodities are spot and futures prices. The spot price is a physical commodity that is changing hands for today, and a future price is a contract for delivering a set amount of the physical commodity some time in the future.

For most individuals, trading physical commodities is not an option, unless that individual has thousands of bushels of corn or a few thousand gallons of crude oil. To make it more practical to invest in commodities, most investors put their money in future contracts or mutual funds that buy futures and other types of forward contracts. Commodity futures do not create direct exposure to actual commodities because future prices are based on the expected future spot price of the commodity that is yet to be delivered. A futures contract is an agreement to buy or sell a quantity of commodity at that future delivery date, and at a price agreed upon when the contract expires.

Often future spot prices will be different from the value of futures contracts because the spot price at a future date is not known; therefore, it must be estimated. Looking at the current spot price, adjusting for interest, and considering seasonable changes and storage expenses, the estimate is created on the spot price.

If the spot prices are expected to be higher, the current futures price will be set higher relative to the current spot price. Lower expected spot prices in the future will reflect in a low current futures price. A buyer benefits when the spot price at maturity turns out higher than was expected and vice versa, rendering the process of spot prices unpredictable.

When a buyer and seller enter into a futures contract, both parties are expected to put up a small amount of cash to affirm the project. No money is exchanged between them at that time, and the cash is exchanged at the end of the contract. When an investor rolls a futures contract from one month to the next, he or she is hoping to benefit from a new price that may be more beneficial.

Individual Commodities

If the timing is right, a good deal of money can be made investing in individual commodities. In the past 50 years, two major runs in commodity prices have taken place. The first occurred in the 1970s during high inflation years; the second happened in the first decade of the twenty-first century. Commodity prices for the other years were normally characterized by flat or falling values.

As a result, there is little chance of making money in these two commodities. Run-ups that happened in the 1970s and 2000s resulted in a great demand for investments benchmarked to individual commodities, something with which mutual fund companies were happy to comply.

Oil

The Net Asset Value (NAV) of the U.S. Oil Fund investment reflects the performance of the spot price of West Texas Intermediate light and sweet crude oil.

The performance of investments in West Texas Intermediate crude futures, tracked by iPath® GSCI Crude Oil Total Return Exchange Traded Note (ETN) tracks, that are non-leveraged, and would be earned through an investment of collateral assets in treasuries.

ETNs are characteristically debt-linked instruments that trade like exchange-traded funds; the difference is that ETNs do not hold a stake in a commodity or commodities futures. Instead, they are senior debt notes from Barclays PLC, in which Barclays promises to pay the exact return of the underlying commodity index.

Gold and Silver

An investor can access the gold market without having to take physical delivery of the gold in several ways. One method is through streetTRACKS Gold Share, which gives investors the opportunity to buy and sell their gold interest through the trading of a security on a regulated stock exchange. In this trust, gold and issues exchange tradeable shares in exchange for deposits of gold. Gold is then distributed in connection with redemptions from those securities.

Each ETF represents one-tenth an ounce of gold. With more than $6 billion invested in the fund by 2006, streetTRACKS Gold Shares is the world's largest private owner of bullion.

iShares Comex Gold Trust equates to one-tenth of a troy ounce of gold, with the Bank of New York valuing the gold on a daily basis of that day's announced Comex settlement price for the spot month gold futures contract. By 2006, there were more than $800 million invested in this fund.

Gold TRAKRS is a non-traditional futures contract that trades on the Chicago Mercantile Exchange, providing investors with an alternative way to gain exposure on the spot price of gold. One difference between Gold TRAKRS and traditional futures contracts is that investors are required to post 100 percent of the TRAKRS market value at the time of purchase.

iShares Silver Trust is based on silver, and each share is equal to ten ounces of silver. JPMorgan Chase operates this trust, with the silver held in the Bank of England. By 2006, there were $900 million invested in this fund.

Commodities Indexes

There are four popular indexes for measuring commodity futures prices: Goldman Sachs Commodity Index, Dow Jones-AIG Commodity Index, Commodity Research Bureau Index, and the Rogers International Commodity Index.

Though they are called indexes, most of the those listed are not indexes, but rather are considered to be well-managed investment strategies. While some index providers will change the weighting of the commodities based on the provider's opportunity, others will do an annual rebalancing that takes into account changes on the global commodity production and consumption level. Others make regular adjustments to the weighting in accordance with rules set well in advance.

Many index providers have also engineered their indexes to take advantage of the large spikes in energy and metal prices in the past decade.

Goldman Sachs Commodity Index

Formed in 1869 by Marcus Goldman, this company pioneered the use of commercial paper for entrepreneurs and was invited to join the New York Stock Exchange in 1896. At this time, Samual Sachs, Goldman's son-in-law, joined the company and created the current name.

In 1929, Goldman Sachs launched the Goldman Sachs Trading Corporation, a closed-end mutual fund. After the 1929 stock market crash, the fund failed, and the reputation of the company was hurt for several years. The firm opened its first international office in London in 1970 and, in the 1980s, it acquired J. Aron & Company, a commodities trading firm.

Come 1985, it underwrote the public offering of the Real Estate Investment Trust that owned the Rockefeller Center, the largest REIT in history. In 1999, the firm went public after years of debate, offering only 22 percent of the company to non-partner employees.

The Goldman Sachs Commodity Index was created in 1991 and is considered the most heavily followed commodity index in the world. It is world-production-weighted, resulting in the quantity of each commodity in the index determined by the average value of production in the past five years of data. This index uses the price of 24 commodities based on overall market value, with all 24 made up of six energy products, five industrial metals, eight agriculture products, three livestock products, and two precious metals. The index generates a high energy weighting because oil dominates the commodity markets. As a result, a small rise in the price of crude oil has a significant effect on the Goldman Sachs Commodity Index.

Dow Jones-AIG Commodity Index

Created in 1998, this fund has a large following among institutional investors. The index derives its value from 20 commodities based on the combination of global production and average trading volume during the most recent five-year period. These weightings are adjusted once per year and put into effect in early January. No commodity sector can start the year with more than a 33 percent position, and no single group component can be more than 15 percent of the group, or 2 percent of the index.

Reuters/Jefferies CRB Index

This was the only commodity firm that had good records of historic commodity prices over a 50-year period. The index was an equal-weighted benchmark of 20 commodities, but the practice caused problems in the past few years, and the index was left far behind while other commodity indexes boomed with energy prices after 2002.

In 2005, the Reuters Group affiliated with Jefferies Financial Products and put a significant holding in energy. Crude oil was given a 23 percent position, and 16 percent more was spread between gasoline, heating oil, and natural gas.

Deutsche Bank Liquid Commodity Index

Created in 2003, this index was intended to reflect the performance of a handful of the most liquid and globally traded commodities, each with set weights. Crude oil allocation is 35 percent, heating oil is 20 percent, aluminum is 12.5 percent, gold is 10 percent, and corn and wheat are 11.25 percent. These percentages are noted for being in proportion to historic levels of the world's production and stocks.

This index uses rebalancing, which is unusual for a commodity index; a rebalancing occurs in the positions in energy futures (crude oil and heating oil) each month; the other four contracts are rebalanced once a year.

Rogers International Commodity Index

The Rogers International Commodity Index was created in 1998, basing its strategy on the monthly closing prices of a fixed-weight portfolio of the nearby futures. It contains 35 different contracts, representing zinc, nickel, lumber, oats, barley, azuki beans, wool, rubber, and silk.

Standard and Poor's Commodity Index

This index was introduced in 2001 and tracks 17 commodities that trade on the U.S. exchanges. Liquidity is measured by the level of open interest held by traders on which the weighing is based. Rather than using arithmetic methodology, Standard and Poor's uses geometric methodology to calculate the index. This lowers the volatility but creates higher trading costs, and double counting is also part of the index, which lowers the weighting of commodities that are upstream from another commodity in the index. This is also the only index that excludes gold.

Merrill Lynch Commodity eXtra Index

This index is a relatively new one, coming into being in 2006 to give an accurate representation of the value of commodities in the global economy. Commodities indexes characteristically hold futures contracts that must be rolled over occasionally, with funds normally holding soon-to-expire "front-month" contracts and rolling over to "second-month" contracts upon expiration. The Merrill Lynch Commodity eXtra Index frequently holds the "second-month" contract and rolls it into the "third-month" contract.

Lehman Brothers Commodity Index

This index measures the performance of commodities in a diverse mix of future contracts. The Lehman Brothers Commodity Index contains 20 commodities in four major sectors: energy, metals, agriculture, and livestock. The weights of the index, as of 2006, were 56 percent energy, 23 percent metals, 18 percent agriculture, and 3 percent livestock.

Total Return Indexes

Total return indexes are designed to replicate fully collateralized commodity futures. The total return price equates to the price return on the commodity futures added to the difference in price between old futures contracts that are near expiration.

Total Return Commodity Funds

It is vital to remember that the published returns of the indexes do not reflect the returns of investors in mutual funds that benchmark said indexes. Each managed fund of commodities has annual management fees and sales commissions to buy in, and the costs for these can be quite expensive. Some fees reach 2 percent per year in addition to a sales charge that reaches nearly 6 percent. Tracking errors in commodities are also higher than those of stocks and bonds, and fund managers must battle the cost and timing of rolling on contract date to try and maintain continuity in the index.

Currency Funds

As the U.S. dollar falls, investors may often wish they could trade in a fund that could make money from the changing exchange rate.

Thanks to the implementation of currency funds, it is possible now, helping to provide a bright spot for some during a disappointing economic situation.

It has not always easy to make money from the movements of foreign currencies. Investors had used futures contracts, but that required a separate brokerage account and required a large amount of money. Often, investors found that single future contracts, each holding as much as 125,000 Euro, were just too large an investment to handle.

Investors could also go through Wells Fargo or American Express to buy small amounts of foreign currency, but these transaction costs were high. On top of that, investors did not receive any of the interest on the currency.

Traditionally, banks and brokerages have dominated currency markets, but now, individual investors are seeing the opportunity to invest in the currency markets through exchange-traded funds (ETFs), whose sole objective is to reflect the price of the currency being held by the fund. While some interest is paid in the account, and money is held in trust, the main reason investors want to use currency funds is the currency exposure.

The first currency ETF was launched by Rydex Investments on the New York Stock Exchange in December 2005; six more ETFs were added in June 2006. Each of these funds holds a different foreign currency with an overseas branch of JPMorgan Chase Bank. This currency fund was designed to rise in value when the euro strengthened relative to the U.S. dollar, and to fall when the euro weakened.

As previously mentioned, Rydex Investments added six more currency-based exchange traded funds to the market in the launch of the CurrencyShares series of funds on the New York Stock Exchange. Those ETFs, which were the

Australian dollar, British pound sterling, Canadian dollar, Mexican peso, Swiss franc, and Swedish krona, were created to track the price movements of world currencies. These new ETFs worked on the same principles as the first currency fund.

However, it is important to remember that there is no cash income from currency funds — that is not their objective. If investors decide to sell the shares after a fund's currency has strengthened relative to the U.S. dollar, he or she will have a monetary gain. With these new funds, investors can benefit from the trend of the U.S. dollar's decline.

There was a time when giant institutional investors, like banks, dominated currency markets. This is no longer the case, and in spite of the risks, no individual could play in the currency market as well as an institutional investor.

For instance, those who invested in the Canadian Dollar Trust gained a large amount on their investment when the dollar rose almost 25 percent in 2007. The Euro Trust also gained 18 percent over the past year. Dividends are paid based on foreign interest rates, with the Euro Trust paying 3.77 percent, the Australian Dollar Trust paying 6.13 percent, and the British Pound Trust paying 5.43 percent.

Currency funds resemble savings accounts, as they hold cash and invest it with banks to gain interest. When it is measured against foreign currency, the shares will not gain or lose much value. For example, a share worth 100 euro now will be worth the same next month or next year. This is the main difference between currency funds and foreign bonds. Foreign bond value moves up and down, even in their local currency.

As with any type of fund, diversification is useful. If investors have foreign stocks in their portfolio that give exposure to high growth areas in the world, or have their savings in a foreign currency, it can protect them in case the dollar falls.

Of course, investing in currency funds will not mean high returns on a constant basis. A small increase in the dollar's value can cause money to be lost in funds, as currency funds are anything but a sure thing. Nevertheless, by understanding the risks, buying currency funds with a small portion of an investor's cash holdings can play a useful role in a portfolio.

Currency-based Indexes

These types of indexes reflect the performance of a particular currency and can be used to hedge an index against a currency exposure or attribute the performance of an index to a currency factor.

Where Do We Go from Here?

After taking the time to understand the concept, history, advantages and types of index funds, we are ready to learn how to invest in them and how to construct a portfolio.

The funds that were detailed in this chapter are not the most popular. In the case of currency funds, they are relatively new to the game. By understanding all the types of funds available, including currency and commodity funds, the road to understanding how to put together a proper portfolio can be realized.

Commodities are some of the most popular types of investments for investors worldwide because they are items we all use. Look at an average day to understand how much commodities play a vital role in people's lives: The cotton sheets that were picked in the American South in the average bed; the clothing that was made in the Far East; the toast made from wheat in the Midwest and the glass of milk from a dairy farm in Wisconsin. Cars might be made in Mexico and driven downtown using the gas that was pumped out of the Middle East.

These are items we all need regularly and, with the exception of oil, can be manufactured and used repeatedly. Commodities are a thriving market, whether investing in stocks or index funds.

The same is true with currency funds, which allow investors to measure gains and losses against their native currency. But the money you make can easily be taken away — which is true with anything in the stock market.

Historically, it has been difficult for investors to participate in commodities and currencies unless they were part of a large investment firm. Thanks to the advent of the index fund, however, the individual investor can now become more involved. It may not be at the same level as the large companies, banks, and brokerages, but investors can at least gain a piece of the currency and commodity pies.

The benefit of index funds, as made evident throughout the past six chapters, is that they are an innovative way for anyone to try investing without the monumental risk of active investing or stock picking. Investors can enjoy the security of the fund and the joys of the stock market without the worry.

As a result, index funds have revolutionized the stock market and finance industry. For many investors, the idea of having the stock market all to themselves was an attractive option, and by buying large stocks, they could hold onto that power. Yet the advent of the index fund better distributed the power, and the stock market was drastically changed

It is of little surprise that though the stock market slowly climbs over time, the index fund exploded from one fund in the early 1970s to hundreds of funds 25 years later. Everything seems to have an index fund attached to it now — from industry sectors and commodities to currencies and morality.

2004
2005
Valor 1076509

Section 3

The first thing a potential investor must understand when beginning to put together a portfolio is that it all comes down to planning, setting goals, and understanding the risks involved.

Planning for the future is imperative to any form of success. A disorganized and poorly constructed portfolio ends up costing the chance to benefit from the index fund revolution. Furthermore, goals must be set for a portfolio, and these goals tie-in directly with a plan for the future.

Goals are the markers for a future; they are the benchmarks one must meet throughout an investment life. To set goals and plan a promising future, one must understand the risk that comes with investments.

Risk is essential to the stock market, though. As seen several times in this book, the higher the risk, the greater the reward. To determine how much risk to take, however, one must determine what kind of reward is desired.

Putting together a portfolio involves several considerations that will be touched on in this section. But that is only the beginning. Throughout the life of an investment portfolio, it will be constantly retooled.

This is what compiling a portfolio is all about. It means working to succeed in reaping as much reward as possible with as little risk as possible. Still, remember that it is there is no such thing as getting rich quick. The only way to ensure reliable success for any investor is gradual growth, complete with low risk and average earnings. It takes time to put together a large portfolio base.

Once the planning process is complete, an investor is ready to begin implementing and managing. It may seem overwhelming considering the amount of knowledge it takes to understand the entire industry. But the beauty of index funds is that they are easy to use and are meant to help the average person make money in the stock market. As has been said numerous times in this book, it is not the point of the index fund to beat the market, but to simply mirror it — that is where its true power lies.

Not everyone will have the time to manage their portfolio, and with that comes the dreaded realm of procrastination — see Chapter Nine. One must be sure to get the most out of an investment portfolio, and procrastination will take away from this goal. Many will decide to take a chance on an investment advisor who will keep a portfolio in order for a small fee.

But if done right — after extensive planning and developing — it can be simple to manage a portfolio.

MRC
M−
M+
$249.00
$40.00
$30.00
$4.00
$103.00
$40.00
$0.00
$249.00
$289.00
$319.00
$323.00
$426.00

7

Planning & Setting Goals

"The victory of success is half won when one gains the habit of setting goals and achieving them. Even the most tedious chore will become endurable as you parade through each day convinced that every task, no matter how menial or boring, brings you closer to fulfilling your dreams."

- Og Mandino

We all have goals in our life. These may be goals that define what we want to do with our lives, goals that are associated with our job, or simple goals such as trying to get all of our errands done in one day. Of course, the point of goals is to meet them, else risk a sense of failure.

With this in mind, try to set goals that are achievable. Do not set goals that are going to be impossible to achieve; by knowing how the index fund market works, it is more realistic to be able to set achievable goals that will work for you.

Index funds are one of the safest ways for an individual to invest in the stock market. They combine diversity with low-risk and average gain. But that does not mean that losing money cannot happen. Setting goals too high in the financial market makes you more likely to suffer — both emotionally and financially.

There are several steps in setting index fund goals for your own portfolio, and perhaps the most important is understanding risk.

Risk

Risk is inevitable in day-to-day lives and is what helps us strive to be more than what we are. We may risk financial difficulty by quitting our day job to pursue the ambiguous dream job, but the reward could be far greater in terms of our emotional happiness. We may risk obtaining a loan for a vehicle we desire, or take the risk of asking someone out on a date. No matter the risk, with it comes reward, and it is important to understand the correlation between the two.

Rewards motivate lives. We envision the rewards of working hard at the office: higher pay, a better office, and more prestige in our position. We look to the reward of seeing another person smile when we help them through their day. No matter the reward, it must come with at least a small risk.

As has been said many times in this book, the greater the risk, the greater the reward. We already know that the risk in index funds is small to average. Correspondingly, our reward is typically the same.

For an investment in the stock market to prove fruitful, risks must be taken. That being said, too much risk means the possibility of losing more than you gained. Stock pickers frequently gamble with others' money. Going this route can reap rewards if luck brings you a fortunate stumble on the right stock, but it can also mean you could potentially suffer.

As a result, a lower risk in a stock portfolio is a smarter move. The lower the risk, the higher the probability that you will be able to ride out any storm on the stock market waters, including a bear market that leaves many stock pickers' portfolios in ashes.

The Three Factor Risk Model

As we learned previously, William Sharpe had identified two forms of risk in the stock market: systematic and unsystematic risk. Nevertheless, his one-factor model of risk explained only 70 percent of the returns on the stock market. His one-factor model stated that the amount of a portfolio invested in stocks was the most important factor in determining stock return.

In 1992, Eugene Fama and Kenneth French worked on a three-factor model to describe how risk and return on stocks correlated. By evaluating data from 1964 to 1926 and beyond, they extended what Sharpe had concluded, hoping to describe why differences exist among returns for stock asset classes over long periods of time. This would allow them to identify the remaining 30 percent of returns that were not explained by Sharpe.

They concluded there were three risk factors — size, market, and value — that work together to pinpoint the sources of investment risk. This new three-factor risk model explained 95 percent of the returns on the stock market in the United States and elsewhere.

They found that investors' performances in comparison with other investors and the stock market depended mostly on the percentage of stocks, which is the market factor held in a portfolio, and also the amount of small and book-to-market ratio stocks in a portfolio.

The Market Risk Factor

The market risk factor is determined by how much of the portfolio is invested or exposed to stocks. If there is a higher exposure, there is a higher return in terms of U.S. Treasury bills.

The Size Risk Factor

Exposure to this form of risk comes from how much of the portfolio is invested in smaller company stocks.

Characteristically, small company stocks have small market capitalization, so these are perceived as a riskier investment than larger company stocks because of lower market capitalization and fewer financial resources. Small companies also have more trouble surviving economic difficulties than the larger more established companies. Again — higher risk means higher return.

In the past 80 years, small company stocks have outperformed large company stocks by 3.13 percent per year. Of course, getting those high returns comes with a greater risk.

The Value Risk Factor

The value risk factor is the amount of exposure a portfolio has to low-priced stocks; it is measured by looking at the stocks' book-to-market value ratio.

The book value, or net income, is compared with the market value (price per shares), multiplied by the number of outstanding shares the company has. If the market price is less than the book value, then the book-to-market value is above one.

Exposure to this is determined by how many high book-to-market stocks there are in a portfolio. The bigger the value of the book-to-market value, the higher the expected return will be. Low book-to-market value stocks are growth stocks and are favored by many investors because they are less risky than the other types of book-to-market stocks. On average, value stocks, or high book-to-market stocks, outperform growth stocks. In a study done in 1987, the investment performance of 29 growth and 29 value stocks were analyzed. The study found that between 1981 and 1985, value stocks outperformed growth stocks 282 percent to 182 percent, despite the growth stocks being from companies that were healthier in every way, including return on equity and sales, and even though the value stocks represented poorly managed companies, bad images, and low profitability.

Understanding Risk Tolerance and Avoidance

Risk tolerance is understanding the level of risk an investor can handle without failure. If investors know their level, then they do not go above it; if they do, they may not be able to recover quickly enough from the financial repercussions.

One way that risk tolerance is calculated by financial advisors is through an investment questionnaire. Many different financial advisors use this method because it allows them to understand not only the level of risk tolerance, but also what a client is looking for in a stock investment.

Conversely, while the questionnaire can help a financial advisor find the right type of investment, they can also be inaccurate and inadequate because they may push investors into taking more risk than they can handle. It is not surprising to understand why this happens, as most firms make higher commission and fees when they are investing in aggressive investments instead of low-risk investments.

A good risk tolerance questionnaire can be found at the Vanguard Group online at **www.Vanguard.com**.

Once one understands his or her individual risk tolerance, he or she can begin to practice risk avoidance, which is the process by which you prevent yourself from assuming unnecessary risk that could be detrimental to financial well-being.

It is easier said than done, as people tend to gravitate toward risk; it is part of our curiosity about the human condition and the world around us. The same is true in the stock market. Investors know the risks are too great. But they can choose to go too far in their investment anyway — either through pride or greed — and lose everything.

Risk avoidance must be practiced by any prudent investor. Knowing your risk tolerance is one thing; not surpassing it is another. Risk avoidance has to be a conscious decision to avoid crossing the tolerance level.

As you progress through the stock market, your risk tolerance and avoidance will change. Early on, a new investor may take greater risks because any disruptions in the stock market will eventually even out over the course of an investing life. As time goes on, and as money is inserted into a bank account, fewer risks might be taken because there is more to lose. At this point, a portfolio can change from one of growth orientation to one of wealth preservation. And avoiding unnecessary risk means having less anxiety in case of a bear market.

It is natural for many investors to overestimate their risk tolerance and feel that they can handle more than the average investor. As a result, they raise their risk level, hoping for a bigger return.

Nevertheless, stock market declines can happen, such as those in 1929, the bear markets from 1973 to 1974 and 2000 to 2002, and the Black Monday of 1987. All these examples demonstrate a downturn in the market, with individual investors selling their stocks in an effort to stop their own financial bleeding, making the situation even worse. There is a lot of risk in the market, and most investors cannot handle it — regardless of what they say about their risk tolerance.

All About Control

In a portfolio, ones must understand that control over three areas of the investment is essential:

- The Cost
- The Risk
- The Taxes

Costs are one of the easiest items to control because this involves a conscious decision. Knowing all your portfolio expenses will likely result in investment purchases that have a lower cost.

For example, there would be little point in purchasing a high-cost mutual fund if invests in the same securities as a low-cost index fund. Why pay the extra fees when the reward is going to be the same in the case of a low-cost index fund?

You control risk when you allocate the amount of money between your bond and stock indexes. The decision to have more short-term bonds in a portfolio renders a relatively low risk.

Depending on their financial security, it is common among investors to take control of their investments. If financial security is high, they actually may reduce the risk in an effort to maintain that security. Taxes can also be controlled by the investor through estate planning and management techniques. One effective way to control taxes is to invest in tax-friendly investments like tax-sheltered retirement accounts.

Some factors affecting a portfolio are completely out of our control, including the markets themselves, political situations, and governance. Consequently, it is prudent to control as much as possible. Start with taxes, risk, and costs so that the things you cannot control will not overwhelm you.

Think Ahead

Most people who spend most of their life as a working employee look to the light at the end of the tunnel called "retirement." For those who do not think ahead, retirement can be a stressful or nonexistent affair because the funds simply are not there. But by thinking about investing for retirement, one can build up a successful future.

Making an investment decision that will aid you in retirement is an important one, but it will only work if you stick with it. Keep the decision in mind for years and put a specific amount of money into investments to meet a goal. When looking at those investments, ask some important questions:

1. How much money should I invest in the safety of bonds?

2. How much money should I risk in the stock market?

To find the answers to those vital important questions, look at creating a planning model. A planning model should help aid in determining your current financial situation, as well as future goals and needs. It would be easy to simply go by a common model that everyone can use, but the truth is that everyone's retirement goals are different, and that means everyone will have different planning models.

On average for most retirees, the amount of income retirees need equates to about 85 percent of the preretirement income because income taxes are lower. Pension checks have no tax, social security, or Medicare payments deducted.

Where to Begin

Investing begins with the individual. One must know what your money can do for you, during your life and afterward for any heirs to ensure financial security, a comfortable retirement, and security for children and grandchildren.

With these goals in mind, it is up to you to make them happen. Many individual investors will have these goals, yet many will not do what is needed to ensure those goals are met. Often, investment portfolios are poorly constructed with mismatched stocks and bonds, and funds gathered through a mixed-up variety of sources.

Before your first investment is made, however, it is best to make a solid investment plan that you have committed to in writing. Hang it in your office as a constant reminder. This small step will help keep you on track by preventing you from picking up various stocks and funds simply because you heard positive news about them that day.

The first priority to establish when building an investment plan is to figure out how much money you currently need to feel secure. After that, determine how much money you will spend each year in retirement. When you are 30, it is difficult to know exactly what you are going to spend each year for the next 40 years. A good estimate, at this point, is to aim for 70 to 90 percent of what you currently spend. Remember, when you are 70, it is unlikely that you will still be taking care of car or home payments, which eat up a substantial portion of monthly and yearly income.

By examining these issues, you can satisfy your current financial needs and forecast the amount needed to begin building your retirement years.

The Goals

A financially healthy retirement is the goal of those who plan on living a comfortable life after the age of 65. Naturally, that means that most of the investment packages are intended to be used as a way to ensure financial security decades down the road.

As already stated, a retiree will not require as much income because there are not as many taxes that need to be repaid. So, when setting financial goals for retirement, start by looking at the current monthly budget.

It is possible to have a large nest egg that will maintain the life you currently enjoy and require you to pay fewer taxes. Many couples will retire with a nest egg of more than $1 million or $1.5 million and enjoy the life they are accustomed to. If this is the case, a couple could live on $75,000 per year for 20 years, which should be more than enough.

When deliberating over an investment package, plan to have $1.5 million in savings by the age of 65. If you are considering placing money into a bank account without considering interest, then at the age of 25, one needs to put in $37,500 a year; at age 45, it goes up to $75,000 per year. This is a major amount of money to deposit each year; hence, it is wise to establish an investment package that can create gains on your investment.

While that $1.5 million investment works in our current year, it could be different down the road for the retired couple that ends up saving that much. Inflation is the enemy of the retirement fund, and a 3 percent inflation rate over the course of 20 years for a couple hoping to retire actually amounts to more than $3 million.

Investment Return

Once you know you need $3 million in savings for retirement, you can begin to create the savings plan that will help you get there.

For example, if you are 45 years old and are planning for a retirement amount of $3 million with $500,000 saved, what is the rate of return you need to achieve that goal?

Knowing your investment return will help you formulate what you need to invest in over the course of your portfolio's life. Normally, when you have a sizeable savings, a sizeable retirement goal in mind, and 20 years before retirement, you will need at least a 7 percent return on your investments.

This type of return can be reasonably expected on a portfolio that is diversified enough, including both stock and bond index funds. That being said, there is no guarantee that you can to achieve that. Some years may yield a 12 percent rate of return; other years may be 3 percent.

We have praised the importance of diversification in your stock portfolio throughout the book, and here is where it truly matters. By having a large amount of diversification, with the target of a 7 percent investment return, you should be able to maintain a constant percentage figure through the years of 7 percent. Planning for a constant return of 10 percent is simply not possible. You may achieve it on occasion, but expecting to achieve it on a regular basis for 20 consecutive years is unlikely.

Projecting Index Fund Returns

It may sound contradictory to previous chapters to say it is possible to forecast index fund returns. After all, we spent a large portion of the book describing how you cannot predict what the stock market is going to do from one day to the next. Actually, a large basis of index funds is based on the facts we discussed earlier in the book.

There are essentially three ways to try to determine index fund returns in the future, but remember: It is impossible to predict what will happen in the stock market; you can only forecast what might happen.

The three methods look at mathematical models using current interest rates, tax rates, and other factors that combine past market data with conservative estimates. All three models take into consideration the history of the stock market and its trends, in an effort to forecast what will happen. This is different than stock pickers and active investors, who look at tips and rumors to pick the stocks

As Julian Barnes once said about history:

> *"Does history repeat itself, the first time as tragedy, the second time as farce? No, that's too grand, too considered a process. History just burps, and we taste again that raw-onion sandwich it swallowed centuries ago."*

Essentially, history does repeat itself, and that can be used to get a slim understanding of what the market might do; this by no means is firm and, most likely, you will find it is almost impossible to forecast. Because you will never know exactly what the market will do, it is best to be conservative in your estimates.

When you are looking at stock market history, you should focus on the past 40 years or so. 40 years should give you enough ups and downs to be able to see any trend that may have developed in the past. Stock prices move in bull and bear markets, and there will be several in a span of 40 years.

From 1967 to 1983, there was a low-level, long-term bear market caused by the stagflation economy, the energy crises of the 1970s, and unemployment of the early 1980s.

Look at the Black Monday Crash of 1987, the October 27, 1997 mini-crash, and the stock market downturn of 2002.

Another bear market occurred from 2000 to 2002, along with a current downturn in the market that began in 2006.

Those events correspond with the bull markets, which in the past 40 years looked like this:

The bull market of the 1990s saw the fastest growth of the global financial markets in history. It was the longest bull market in stock market history. And the United States was in a bull market, with brief upsets, from 1983 to the late '90s.

Few would have thought that the markets would have their most amazing growth from 1983 to more than a decade later, after a severe downturn before that. But though few events can be predicted, what can be done is the analysis of what happened during those times and how people reacted. The stock market cannot be predicted — but people can be.

Studies have found that since 1880, there have been four major stock market trends, each lasting roughly 30 years. These results show that 30 years is equivalent to one generation. People will often have a bear market early in their lives while they are investing in small amounts, but they may be in a bull market by the end of their lives. While this is not always true, many generations will see roughly two waves in their lifetime.

For example, the most recent wave, beginning in 1982, came early in the careers of the baby boomers, who were just beginning their investments. Most were in their early to late 30s and had little money to invest. The people who truly benefited from the bull market that occurred in the 1980s and '90s were the baby boomers' parents, who, if they invested early and correctly, benefited from an amazing market that was paying dividends on their investments.

The baby boomers are nearing their bull market, which could come within a few years. For those younger than the Baby Boomers, say Generation X, they are only now getting into the stock market and will likely have to wait until the next 30-year cycle to benefit.

Over a long period of time, it is universally accepted that stocks will outperform bonds because there is more risk inherent in stocks, while bonds have more of a risk than money market funds and will, therefore, outperform stocks over the years.

Selecting the Portfolio through Asset Allocation

We addressed asset allocation in a previous chapter, and now it becomes relevant. How you want to divide everything is your choice. Some will go for a 60 percent U.S. stock index fund, combined with a 40 percent corporate bond index fund. A balanced mix ensures you do not suffer if the market becomes a bear, resulting in a lower return on investment if you have invested heavily in one sector of the market.

Thus, it is a good idea to split a portfolio between a U.S. stock and a corporate bond index fund. A 60 percent stock and 40 percent bond allocation is the normal method, as it is a safe way to provide a decent return that can give you the 7 percent investment return.

When you do create your portfolio using asset allocation, do not forget about risk tolerance. Make sure the asset allocation reflects what your goals are and that you are not placing yourself in an unnecessary risk situation that may affect retirement savings.

Remember that you will be paying fees for your index funds. These fees will be low, but that will affect how much is given back on your investment. If you want a 7 percent return on your portfolio, shoot for 7.5 percent.

When doing an asset allocation, look at two varied methods: aggressive and conservative.

Aggressive Allocation

Aggressive allocation involves having something like 70 percent in a stock index and 30 percent in a bond market index, a method used because investors would be trying to achieve as much gain as possible in a short period of time. This can be an especially risky maneuver when the stock market has a bad year while the bond market has a good year. If a couple had an asset allocation of 70/30 for stocks and bonds, then they could assume to lose $12,000 on a $300,000 investment, which would be disastrous. If the stock market continued at a bad pace for a few years, as it did from 2000 to 2002, the couple would lose tens of thousands of dollars in value on their portfolio. This means a retired couple would need to sell their portfolio; with no other income coming in, they would not be able to maintain their allocation at a high loss rate.

Conservative Allocation

For that same couple enduring the troublesome period between 2000 and 2002, but instead using a 50/50 stock and bond allocation, there is a much greater chance of success. For this couple, through the tough years of the stock market and decent years of the bond market, losses would be only half of what the aggressive allocation investors lost.

This does not mean you should not invest using an aggressive allocation. Again, higher risk means higher reward, and a 70/30 stock and bond allocation means taking a greater risk. If the investor with that type of portfolio hits a bull market in which stocks do well, like the super-bull market of the 1990s, they will benefit significantly from taking that risk. On the other hand, for many, there is simply too much risk in using that form of allocation without enough financial preparation.

Do not risk losing what you have earned for your retirement because you of needless greed. You will use your portfolio as your retirement investment for 40, 30, or 20 years. You have plenty of time to accumulate funds at a slow pace with a smaller risk of losing everything you have worked so hard to attain.

Moving On

There is more to putting together an index fund portfolio than just picking the index funds you desire. One must understand how the future will be affected by your choices today. Be able to plan ahead to foresee what will happen and understand how the market is going to fluctuate over the course of your life. Decide if you are going to invest in growth stocks or value stocks, depending on what point you are at in your life, and be able to understand the type of risk you are willing to take.

8

Putting Together a Portfolio

"If stock market experts were so expert, they would be buying stock, not selling advice.

- Norman Augustine

"It will fluctuate."

- J.P. Morgan, when asked what the stock market will do.

Creating an index fund portfolio is not a one-step task; there are many avenues to it, as we have seen in past chapters. From this path, you can gain a clear understanding of what you want at the end of your investment career, which normally comes after retirement. You know you must aim for a certain amount of money in the future to maintain the standard of living you currently, or hope to, enjoy.

Also, with any portfolio, know that you must consider, as always, risk. With portfolios, it spells the difference between success and failure.

A portfolio high in risk will return higher profits when the risk pays off, and despair when it does not. A portfolio low in risk will return low profits, but over the years, those profits will amount to more money.

Asset allocation will help measure risk, with a 60/40 or 50/50 stock/bond mix being the most conservative style for asset allocation. Remember — do not take on a greatly risky situation.

Stocks or Bonds?

As we saw in the previous chapter, a decision must be made regarding how much money to allocate to stocks, and how much to allocate to bonds. While the risky move will take a heavy stock presence in their portfolio, the less risky will take more bonds. This decision will make a great difference in the success of your portfolio and will account for more than 90 percent of the performance the portfolio has over time.

We know that stocks pay off more over time but come with a higher risk, while bonds do not. When choosing between the two, look at your own personality, how long you plan on having the portfolio, and the types of gains you want over time. Again, often a 60/40 split is the best option.

Life's Little Stages

When putting together a portfolio, decisions reflect upon one's own age group. In his book, *All About Index Funds*, Richard A. Ferri devised a guide describing the stages of life: Early Savers, Mid-Life Accumulators, Pre-Retirees and Active Retirees, and Mature Retirees. Let us look at these in more depth.

Early Savers

The early savers range in age from 20 to 39. They are the investors that are just starting their investment portfolio and are unlikely to have a large amount of investment cash. They have few assets, but they make up for it with their drive to succeed in the stock market.

In this stage of their investment life, they do not know exactly what they want in the future; they will likely be trying to accumulate funds for reinvestment or savings. If early savers do the things right initially, they will reap financial rewards in the future.

Early savers will put more importance on a consistent savings plan, rather than the rate of return on their portfolio.

Early savers have an excellent advantage — time. They are still young and are able to handle large-scale financial disruptions more easily. They can suffer a financial blow that seems to destroy their world, but they can weather the storm and wait for better days. Eventually, time will heal their wounds.

Of course, this does not mean they can be reckless with their investments. Consistency is key — early savers should have a 70/30 stock/bond split in their portfolio.

It also would be prudent for them to ensure that no more than 50 percent of their stocks is in the U.S. market. They should try to balance it out with a quarter or so of their stocks in international markets.

Mid-Life Accumulators

These are investors between the ages of 40 and 59 who have settled into a family life and have established careers. They have more money and have accumulated more possessions, including cars and homes. They have a firm grasp on what they want out of life and are beginning to look to the future and what retirement holds for them; they understand the need for a long-term investment plan.

By now they are halfway through their career life, and their salaries are increasing. They have a clear vision of their future and an understanding of how they want their portfolio to reflect that vision. Mid-life accumulators will begin to calculate how much they will need for retirement.

Their portfolio should shift to a 60/40 stock/bond split, showing a less risky attitude toward life. They should also maintain no more than 40 percent in U.S. stocks and about 20 percent in international stocks. This would reflect their need to have more savings with less risk, hence lending them greater diversification in their portfolio.

Pre-Retirees and Active Retirees

Roughly a half-decade before retirement, investors will enter this period of life, but it does not mean they have to retire. It simply means that they have come to the age of retirement. Many will ask themselves if they want to retire, how much money will they have at retirement, and how they will keep from outliving the amount of money they have saved so far. Characteristically, they are between the ages of 60 to 79.

Naturally, at this point, spending becomes more conservative. They do not want to spend too much and jeopardize the lifestyle they have become accustomed to. Here, a major shift in their portfolio occurs, reflecting a new conservative attitude toward their investments. As a result, there will be a marked reduction in the risk of their portfolio, and many will try to eliminate all risks — which is the wrong method.

Once retirement occurs, there will be a change in the portfolio. At this point, there will be no more money added to the portfolio; the money will be coming out to support them. Pre-retirees and active retirees should have a conservative portfolio, reflected in a 50/50 stock/bond mix. The U.S. stock portion should be no more than 35 percent, and the international stock should be about 15 percent.

Mature Retirees

Once reaching this point, which is typically the age of 80 and above, it is best to find someone to manage finances for you. A son or daughter would work best, but you need them to begin well in advance to keep some control over your portfolio. Make sure the designated person is someone who understands your estate and knows what you want for your heirs. This includes knowledge of insurance documents and information about investment accounts.

The conservative nature of the portfolio for the retirees is evident; there is a 40/60 stock/bond split, and on average, there will be 30 percent in U.S. stocks and 10 percent in international stocks.

Taxes

When dealing with your portfolio, you will encounter another word that will help you decide how to allocate assets: asset location.

Asset location differs from asset allocation in that you must determine where you want your assets to rest — in other words, whether you should have taxable assets or not.

Your asset location and asset allocation will work together in your portfolio to give the least risk with the most tax-efficiency.

Taxable Accounts

One of the greatest factors that determines your portfolio performance is how you allocate stocks and bonds, but also keep in mind your tax efficiency. Try to create a low-tax account that will allow you to increase your wealth without having to pay a great deal in taxes. If you want to reduce taxes, focus your account on tax efficient investments.

There are several ways to do this, and using Morningstar is one of them, which reports on the tax efficiency of mutual funds. This information comes at a small annual cost to access their database.

Broad Market Equity Index Funds are tax-efficient because trading is low and there is not large turnover in securities. As mentioned before, exchange-traded funds are also more efficient than open-ended funds, simply by design.

When dealing with bonds in a taxable account, there are several methods to use. Some include putting equity investments in taxable accounts, and fixed-income investments in a non-taxable account.

On the other hand, this strategy is not used by some because investors may have few funds in tax-deferred accounts; the return after taxes on bonds may be higher in a taxable account, and the person may not be able to divide their investments by account type.

If you want to put bonds in a taxable account, look at your last tax return under the 1040 Form labeled "Taxable Income." If it is below $75,000 for singles or $125,000, for couples, invest in a taxable bond index fund and pay taxes on the interest of that bond. If you are above $75,000 or $125,000, invest in a tax-exempt bond index fund.

Placing stocks in a taxable account is dependent on how many index funds you have. John Bogle always said that one fund is all anyone needs, but other experts feel that two or three funds spread across various sectors or regions are best. Your index funds will have low taxes regardless because they are efficient due to low turnover rates.

Non-Taxable Accounts

Having a non-taxable portfolio will be easier than having a taxable one because there is little excess worry about having taxes affect your opinion when compiling your portfolio.

When you place a bond index into a non-taxable account, use a diversified total bond market index fund, then add a high-yield corporate bond fund and a TIPS fund. Do not invest more than 10 percent into a high-yield bond; these come with an enormous amount of risk, and you do not want your portfolio weighted in their favor.

Stocks in a non-taxable account generally are not significantly different from those in a taxable account. One exception is that small-value funds are not suited for non-taxable accounts and should not be put in them because they are not exceptionally tax efficient due to the high turnover.

Rebalancing

In a perfect world, there would be no need to rebalance your portfolio; everything would be constant and there would be no need for fluctuations. But rebalancing a portfolio is necessary to achieve the long-term investment goals you have set.

You can expect to rebalance your portfolio on an annual basis because stocks will regularly vary and the markets will not always stay the same. During a bear market, you may find that your stocks are pulling your portfolio down and you may want to invest more in bonds, thereby shifting your asset allocation to protect your funds.

After a particularly hard market, you may decide to sell some stocks and invest more in fixed-income. This means that if a 70/30 stock/bond were split, you would change to 60/40 to reflect your desire for greater security with less risk.

It may have little to do with bonds and stocks but, rather, more about the sectors, meaning you might move more of your stocks from the American sector to the international sector, perhaps investing more in Brazil or China. This is true with industry sectors as well; you may choose to purchase communication stocks rather than technology stocks.

While there are no tax consequences in rebalancing a nontaxable account, there are taxes in a taxable account. Here are some tips and tricks to ensure you do not lose too much money when rebalancing your taxable account portfolio.

1. Whenever you add money to your account, use that as an opportunity to rebalance the portfolio.

2. If one asset class moves further than another and puts your asset allocation out of balance, only sell the assets that have been in your account for more than 12 months. This is done because it is better to pay the lower long-term capital gain tax rate rather than the high short-term capital gain.

3. Do not reinvest mutual fund income automatically. Instead, choose to let all your income distributions go into your cash account, then manually invest it in the index fund where you feel it is needed.

When you do decide to rebalance, you may want to sell high-performing stocks and invest in lower-end asset classes that are not performing particularly well. This may seem like an odd thing to do, and many investors will choose not to rebalance as a result. But rebalancing has a great deal to do with buying low and selling high, and many investors make the mistake of doing the opposite, which means lower returns for them in the long-run.

Rebalancing your portfolio is often a wise idea during occasions such as:

- When your income changes, either up or down
- When you retire
- When the conditions of your life change, including medical problems
- When your short-term and long-term expenses change
- When the number of your dependents change
- When the investment goals you have set change

It is important to keep a portfolio in tune with your current beliefs, needs, and goals as they change with your life stages.

The 5 Percent/25 Percent Rule

There are important questions: How do you know when to rcinvcst and when your portfolio is off-balance?

On average, if the portfolio moves an absolute 5 percent or 25 percent from its original allocation percentage, you will need to rebalance. You will only use the 5 percent absolutely in certain circumstances, thus if you have an asset class with an allocation of 10 percent or when that asset class' allocation has increased to 15 percent — or fallen to 5 percent — you will use that rule. The 25 percent rule is used differently. Again, if you have an asset class of 10 percent and it has risen or fallen by 2.5 percent (10 percent x 25 percent) to either 12.5 or 7.5 percent, you should rebalance.

On a quarterly or annual basis, you should do the test, which can be applied on these three levels:

1. At the level of equities and fixed income assets
2. At the level of domestic and international asset classes
3. At the level of individual asset classes

All About Planning and Maintaining

Putting together a portfolio can depend strongly on what stage of life you are in and what your life goals are. If you are new to the investing game with many years to flatten out any financial setbacks, you will be more eager to take large risks. If you are 70 and afraid you could end up losing a large portion of your financial security — one that will pay your bills in the retirement — you will want to take few risks.

Yet it is not all about the risk. It also relates with tax efficiency. There are several ways to obtain the greatest efficiency for your dollar, depending on what form of account you decide to put your investments in. You will pay taxes on your portfolio but, by doing it right, you can benefit from consequently paying less.

We also saw in this chapter that once a portfolio is compiled, no matter if it is a 70/30 or 50/50 stock/bond split, you will have to return to it each year and rebalance it to make sure that you continue making money. If you let your portfolio simply go as it will for its entire life, by 20 years down the road, it will be so off-balanced that you will be lucky to make any money at all.

Having a portfolio is not a one-time thing; it is a constant effort to make sure that you pay few taxes, make as much money as you can, and have long-term stability throughout the course of the portfolio. And, of course, the ultimate goal is having enough money to support a financially secure retirement.

9

Managing Your Index Fund Investment

"...ng first things first. Effective management is discipline, ... carrying it out."

-Stephen Covey

"...t of making problems so interesting and their solutions ...ryone wants to get to work and deal with them."

...Hawken, "Growing a Business"

"...works if you first think through your objectives. 90 ...nt of the time you haven't."

- Peter Drucker

Now, we come to the point where it is all about managing the portfolio — effectively, the last step in the road to your index-fund investing future.

In this chapter, you will learn about opening and managing the index fund account you have decided to create. And it all begins with opening the account.

Opening an Index Fund Account

The first step is picking an account that matches your index strategy. This is not always an easy decision, but it is going to be the basis of your investment future for years to come, even affecting how you manage retirement and whether you have enough money to enjoy retirement. It may be one of the most important decisions you make in your life.

Normally, you might start with an open Individual Retirement Account (IRA). IRAs are the easiest accounts to convert into indexing because there are no tax setbacks when you sell investments that you already own.

Still, some of the accounts you have may not be satisfactory or even eligible for indexing. If you work for a company that has a 401(k) plan managed by a bank or brokerage firm, you may suffer from the embedded fees that they attach to their mutual funds. As a result of those fees, they do not offer low-cost index fund options. If this is a problem with your 401(k), talk to the person who administers the plan and explore the option of adding index funds to the 401(k) plan.

Other accounts that may not be transferable include variable annuity accounts. Frequently, these accounts have a sales charge on the back-end that will last as many as ten years. If you just bought one of these from a brokerage or insurance firm, you are likely to be paying that back-end fee right now.

Once the back-end fee load period is over, you can look into other options, such as plans that use low-cost annuity with different index fund options.

Who Will Manage It?

Now that you know the account you want to open, decide on the firm that will manage the index fund for you, typically a mutual fund company that charges low management fees.

Conversely, with that choice comes the disadvantage of a lack of flexibility, as well as limited access because most funds do not allow you to buy the funds of other providers without another purchased account.

There are also discount brokerage firms such as TD Ameritrade, Scottrade, and Charles Schwab that give access to thousands of mutual funds and every stock and bond on the market. Firms like Charles Schwab make managing index funds easier and convenient, although straying to non-Schwab or non-company mutual funds have a disadvantage: When you buy non-Schwab or non-company mutual funds, there is often a commission cost and 12b-1 fee. However, there are so many funds available, you are unlikely to buy from another non-company mutual fund. If you use a full-service broker, exchange-traded funds are also an option.

Paperwork

Once you have found a firm to manage your account, request a new account application and transfer form from them. If you are giving them a check or money to open the account, you do not need to fill out the transfer form. It is, however, important that you obtain the correct type of application; not following instructions properly can cause problems for everyone down the road.

You should be able to find a brokerage house in your area, especially if you live in a major city. When you find a good firm, conduct an in-person meeting with them to ensure you get everything done correctly. Do not worry about being charged for opening an account; this is a free service to all customers, and it is unlikely that you will have to pay to put money into an account.

Fill Out the Forms

Once you have filled out the forms, pass them along to the firm, either in person or through the mail, along with whatever paper work they require.

In an age in which identity theft is common, many people are scared to record personal information on forms. As a result, many forms that go to firms hit roadblocks if the social security number is not listed. However, do not be concerned about sending personal and financial information to the firm; the firms need the information and are bound by law not to divulge anything.

You can also transfer cash and securities by liquidating current investments from your old firm, sending the cash to the new firm, and then liquidating the securities there. If you are investing with a mutual fund company, not a broker, you can only transfer cash.

When doing this, bear in mind commissions and taxes. Look at the cost of selling in your current firm compared to the cost of selling in your new firm to ensure you are paying a minimal amount. If you are transferring in a taxable account, you will have capital gain when you sell a security. If the security is near its 12-month hold period for the long-term capital gains tax rate, wait until it hits 12 months before you decide to liquidate the securities.

Keeping Track

Once everything is settled and you are ready to enter the world of index-fund investing, you must keep track of the paperwork. Most financial systems in large financial companies will allow the securities to move around easily, but if there is a lack of paperwork or oversight, it can lead to problems. Thus, it is important for you to monitor the opening of the account and its assets. Once you send the paperwork, you should get an account number within one week and must wait another three weeks before the transfers are complete.

In the case that you are transferring to another firm, you should ensure you begin the process of selling your assets before you send the paperwork. You will want everything taken care of before all the paperwork goes through in order to streamline the process.

Once everything is set up, do not feel reluctant about calling the firm managing your portfolio; it is up to them to keep you posted on your account.

Procrastination

Most of us have to struggle with procrastination, as it is a serious problem no matter what type of venture you get into for your business. Investors may start putting a strategy together and will promise that they will stick to it, but the process is not always so easy. Most will start to fall away from their strategy as they procrastinate with their portfolio, and others may forget about it completely.

As we have seen in this and previous chapters, making sure your portfolio is successful comes from keeping a constant vigil on it. If your portfolio becomes out of balance, you may lose money, and you could end up surrounded in high-cost investments that you do not want to be in.

Millions of dollars are lost every year by people who procrastinate. Do not head in this direction. Get acquainted with the process and work hard to make sure your portfolio is successful.

Advisors

For investors who cannot maintain a periodic or constant vigilance on their portfolio, there is an alternative solution, and it comes in the form of an investment advisor.

Investment advisors design, manage, tax-manage, and report portfolio progress to the investor for a management fee that can be easily offset by the amount of money you can make with a professional working on the portfolio.

A distinction needs to be made between a financial advisor and a stock picker, however. As we saw in the early chapters, stock pickers are those who take other people's money and invest it for them in stocks that may or may not succeed. As a result, many people lose money when the stock picker fails — as they often they do. Financial advisor are not picking stocks, however; they are managing your portfolio to ensure it is in its best and most profitable condition. They are not buying whatever stocks come to their mind but, rather, are simply ensuring that your balance stays proper and that you do not allow your portfolio to become off-kilter.

Hiring an investment advisor also gives you access to institutional index fund shares, which are low-cost mutual funds that only the clients of an investment advisor have access to.

However, investment advisors do have disadvantages. You cannot guarantee that your advisor will be competent, as they come in all shapes, fees, and sizes, so there is little consistency between them. Do your homework, and make sure the investment advisor you hire has a good track record and does well for his or her clients.

When you do find an advisor that fits what you are looking for, make sure the fee is affordable. On average, the free amounts to about 1 percent of the account size.

Advisor Services

Financial advisors offer several services that can help you in your investment portfolio and retirement future.

First, they can devise an investment plan that fits your needs and can help you understand how to achieve goals through low-cost index fund investing. They will then design a portfolio that will work best for you. Consideration will be given to what you want in your portfolio and your life stage before implementation and management begins. A professional advisor will take much of the guesswork out of it.

Additionally, they can offer consistency in terms of investment strategies. Normally, people switch their strategy every few years, which can excessive, especially during times like the 1990s when growth stocks were popular; a few years later, value stocks became bigger, then investment stocks. As a result, investors completely changed their portfolio based on what the popular trend at that moment was. Investment advisors will not allow this to happen, and they will not chase market fads whenever they come up, allowing you to achieve higher lifetime returns. If you are worrying if the market will collapse, advisors are also there to calm you, help you find peace of mind, and keep you from making emotional investment portfolio decisions.

Lastly, they are there every day, all day. It can be hard for you to juggle management of an investment portfolio while dealing with family, jobs, and other time commitments. An advisor can still take care of your portfolio throughout.

All There Is To It

Managing your portfolio can become easy once you get through the paperwork; it is just a matter of putting everything together.

Decide whether you want an advisor to handle everything. As we discussed, procrastination can cause a great deal of headaches for an investment portfolio, and without care on a regular basis, your portfolio can fall into disarray, creating financial problems if there are high-cost contents that yield few results.

On the flip side, you could over-manage your portfolio and become someone who delves into all the market fads that come along. An advisor can prevent these potentially damaging moves and can be the person who helps you get what you need out of your portfolio at a relatively low cost that can be offset by the higher efficiency your portfolio can have.

All that remains is putting together your portfolio.

The End is a New Beginning

Though originally one of the most ostracized and criticized of all economic revolutions, index funds have proved their merit and have changed the financial world significantly. The fact that the movement was resisted so much by the establishment is a clear indication of how much it would change everything. For those who felt that picking stocks was the way to go, the index fund showed that things could be different.

Through the index fund and its countless pioneers, including Fama, Markowitz, and Bogle, the possibility for an average person to benefit from playing the stock market without the risk and worry that was so often associated with the financial world came into being. Now, people could have low-risk when investing their money. No longer was there a need to listen to "gurus" who tout the greatness of their own strategy.

We have seen how stock picking, time picking, and other techniques fail because of one fact: You cannot predict the market because it is efficient — everything that can be known about it is already out there. There is no way to beat the market; no new information can be garnered to gain a leg up on the competition.

Stock picking and other similar methods may seem like they reward big, and sometimes they do. When someone stumbles on a big stock, they benefit when it pays off, sometimes enough to gain the title of "guru" around Wall Street. But most "gurus" get lucky and ride their past lucky accomplishments. They use those "accomplishments" to convince others to give them their money and let them invest it in the stock market. For the "guru," it is the best of both worlds; they make money, and they do it without losing money. Guessing on the markets, however, is nothing more than a game of chance.

While many will say that index funds are an average way for people to make average money, in a sense, they are wrong. Making average money off index funds is not the point. Average returns, with little risk of guessing wrong and suffering financial ruin, will result in adding average earnings on top of each other for 40, 20, or 10 years. It essentially adds up more and, in the long-run, gives you more money than investing in the stock market through any one of the gimmicky methods we outlined in this book.

Many have worked hard, basing their conclusions on what others have found before them, to pave the long road to the index fund. Taking hundreds of years, dating back to the earliest stock market, it has climbed out of obscurity and into the mainstream to become accepted. It took some time, complete with failure and triumph, to get where it is now, but for many, it was worth the long ride.

Through its diversity, the index fund allows us to invest without much worry. If you do become concerned about one market going down, you can still invest in several, spreading through hundreds or thousands of stocks to ensure you do not risk losing what you have. Through management and planning, you can use the index fund in your portfolio to create the future you want for yourself, your family, and your descendants. They will benefit from your work and your foresight because of your investment strategy.

For anyone who desires low risk and an easier investment, the index fun is effective. No matter what type of sector you decide to invest in, or what you plan to do with your investment, an index fund is the best solution for those who want to benefit from low-risk, average returns with a security that will last for decades.

The index fund could be considered the pinnacle of economic theory and practice, and the fact that you read this book shows that you are one of the forward thinkers who is ready to cast off the incorrect way of investing and begin a new world of safe and proper investing — in the index fund.

Welcome to the Index Fund Revolution.

APPENDIX 1

Low-Cost Index Fund Provider Profiles

Listed here are some of the best low-cost index fund providers you can go through. They will allow you to spend little but reap good rewards for your investment.

Barclays Global Investors

www.ishares.com

A subsidiary of Barclays Bank, the largest corporate money manager in the world with $2.08 trillion under their management umbrella.

The company is headquartered in San Francisco but has several management teams in London, Sydney, Tokyo, Toronto, and other cities around the world.

The company began as a unit of Wells Fargo Nikko and Barclays Bank, which merged in 1996.

The company invented passive index investing strategy for major investors while pioneering the exchange-traded fund business through iShares. Since 2000, the company has seen its active fund management portion of the business grow incredibly.

The iShares fund tracks several bond or stock market indexes, including the American Stock Exchange, the New York Stock Exchange, the Toronto Stock Exchange, the Australian Stock Exchange, and more in Asia and Europe. iShares is the largest issuer of exchanged-traded funds in the entire world.

There are several benefits to purchasing iShares, and one of the biggest is the diversification that it offers. Using iShares helps build a large portfolio at small price. iShares also offers a large amount of categories that give you a broad range of options. Choose from market capitalization style, sector, international, specialty, real estate, fixed income, and precious metals.

The expense ratio of iShares is also low, roughly .09 percent and .75 percent. Turnover is low for iShares, meaning that you can have immense tax-efficiency with your investment.

That being said, if you are looking to invest large amounts of capital, then iShares is excellent, but if you are investing smaller amounts on regularly as part of a dollar cost averaging plan, it may not work well for you because you pay commission to a broker each time you make a purchase. Even with the low-cost, that does add up.

Bridgeway Funds

www.bridgewayfund.com

If having an investment firm committed to ethics is important to you, then Bridgeway Funds is one of the best that you can go through. The company runs on a strong code of ethics, and its CEO has a standard rule that no employee, including himself, can make more than seven times what the lowest employee makes in the company.

The company also operates under low fees and has innovative funds that are the smallest passively managed small-cap fund available.

The company started in 1993 and was founded on strong principles to keep costs down. The company has a lean cost structure that relies on technology and a small, dedicated staff. The company has 11 distinct funds that can be purchased. Despite its advantages as a low-cost investment firm, it does not have a great deal of variety.

Dreyfus

www.dreyfus.com

Founded in 1951, this company was one of the first to create a high-yield mutual fund and advertise to consumers. Based in New York City, the company uses its 50 years of experience to help its investors manage the ups and downs of the market, both in the United States and elsewhere.

They use strategies they have tested over the life of the company to ensure that the investors who use them get the proper focus of asset allocation and diversification.

There are nearly 200 funds that can be invested in, covering several ranges including asset classes, investment styles, market sectors, and market capitalization sizes. The company offers variable and fixed annuities and IRAs and cash management tools that can be used with the Dreyfus Lion Account, which is an all-in-one cash management and asset management account.

Fidelity Group

www.fidelity.com

One of the leading investment firms in the world is Fidelity Group, which provides more than 300 mutual funds. Its services include brokerage services, retirement services, estate planning, wealth management, securities execution and clearance, and life insurance. The company has a strict policy of reinvesting much of what it makes each year toward technology to bring new products and services to investors. Also, its sector Fidelity Management and Research Company employs the largest staff of managers, analysts, and traders in the industry, numbering more than 500.

Some of the tools it provides to the investors that use its services include computer-based research tools that allow instant access anywhere in the world; a linking system between Boston, Hong Kong, London, and Tokyo that tracks all orders and trades; and a state-of-the-art trading desk that gives access to more than 200 brokerage houses with real-time information.

With more than 50 years of experience, Fidelity is considered a world leader in fund management through areas that include stocks, bonds, money markets, high-yield bonds, and asset allocation.

Investors with the company can gain access to Lehman Brothers research and also receive personalized news and information, low commission charges, and no annual fee. Retirement options for clients include IRAs, tax-deferred annuities, mutual funds, planning services, and rollovers.

First Trust

www.ftportfolios.com

One of the leaders in innovative financial services is First Trust Portfolios L.P., which delivers investment products to its clients through comprehensive research that is used to recognize opportunities for investment performance. The investment approach of the company offers equity portfolios including domestic, foreign, sector, strategy, style, hybrid, diversified, and income portfolios that include single-state municipal, national municipal, government, corporate, and high yield bonds.

First Trust also has a strict policy of buying and holding rather than playing the market because they view that method as "emotional investing." They do not use temptation to buy and sell because of stock market volatility, interest rates, inflation, elections, or investment fads; they say they are concerned with long-term rewards more than the day-to-day fluctuations of the markets.

Rydex|SGI

www.rydexfunds.com

Rydex|SGI, formerly Rydex Investments, offers a number of services to the clients who decide to invest through them. They anticipate the needs of investors through continuous innovation and have expressed a commitment to helping investors and investment advisors maximize the value of their tools and strategies for investing.

The company launched the first leveraged benchmark mutual fund ever available to the public among other innovations that include the first short equity and fixed-income mutual funds and intraday pricing.

Currently, the company has $16 billion in assets through 80 mutual funds and exchange-traded funds.

Schwab Funds

www.schwabfunds.com

Schwab Funds portfolios are designed to offer solutions to the needs of the investors who use their services by understanding that diversity is key to success, and they aim to make sure they are as diverse as possible. The company provides the following investment products that allow investors to effectively and efficiently build well-diversified portfolios that offer a range of investment solutions.

1. Fundamental Index Funds were a groundbreaking idea that provided access to the Financial Times Stock Exchange (FTSE) and Research Affiliates (RAFI) Indexes.

2. Real Estate Funds were designed to allow investors to gain access to domestic and international Real Estate Investment Trusts (REIT) and Real Estate Operating Companies (REOCs). The fund managers of the company specialize in real estate category through a global focus that can help decrease the risks associated with the fund.

3. ActiveEquityFundsaredrivenbyindustry-recognized Schwab Equity Ratings that invest in stocks that managers at the company believe will exceed market expectations.

4. Fixed Income Funds are taxable or tax-exempt funds that offer quality bond funds with a large

range of maturities and portfolio volatility, which may generate competitive returns and income.

5. Equity Index Funds are cap-weighted stock benchmarks that capture the performance of the market with low turnover and expenses.

6. Asset Allocation funds offer a mix of stock, bond, and money funds in a single investment, providing a range of assets that will lower the risk of market volatility.

State Street Global Advisors

www.ssga.com

SSGA is part of State Street Corporation, the largest institutional asset manager in the world, with $1.8 trillion in assets under management. The company provides investment strategies to non-profit foundations, businesses, corporations, governments, educational institutions, and religious organizations and is based out of the United States, Europe, Asia, and Australia, employing 1,700 people in 25 locations.

Founded in 1978, it was one of the first companies to offer an index fund. Initially, it offered three: a domestic index, an international index, and a short-term investment fund. By 1989, the company had reached $53 billion in assets under management.

SSGA was a leader in the investment of exchange-traded funds in 1993 when it introduced the S&P 500 SPDR product that trades on the American Stock Exchange. Currently, SSGA is the No. 2 exchange-traded fund manager in the world, behind Barclays.

SSGA launched the first foreign real estate ETF in 2006, allowing investors to access international housing and commercial development markets.

The company now has 46 ETF investment products in the United States, which track international and domestic indexes based on market-caps, investment style, sector, commodity, and industry.

SSGA also partners with Advanced Investment Partners, Asian Direct Capital Management, GovernanceMetrics International, Innovest Strategic Value Advisors, Rexiter Capital Management, Shott Capital Management, SSARIS Advisors, The Tuckerman Group, and Wilton Asset Management to provide local investment strategies for clients.

T. Rowe Price

www.troweprice.com

Founded in 1937, T. Rowe Price is one of the oldest investment management firms in the country. Based in Baltimore, Maryland, the company offers a broad range of mutual funds, sub advisory services, account management, retirement plans, and financial intermediaries, as well as investment tools. The company states that it is mindful of the risks relative to the rewards, and it is their policy to help mitigate unfavorable changes and take advantage of favorable ones. This is done through world-class investment guidance and attentive service.

The company's founder, Thomas Rowe Price, set the focus of the company through his effort to manage investment portfolios and retirement programs. He believed that what was good for the client was good for the firm, choosing to charge a fee based on assets under management rather than commission. Price created the growth-stock style of investing, which has now become one of the most important investment styles of the firm.

Vanguard Group

www.vanguard.com

One of the pioneers in the index fund revolution, the Vanguard Group currently has $1.3 trillion in assets through managing mutual funds and other financial products for investors both abroad and in the United States. The company was founded by John C. Bogle, who is credited with creating the first index fund.

The company is owned by the funds themselves, which is unusual for mutual-fund companies. In the company, each fund puts a set amount of capital toward shared management, marketing, and distribution services. This allows the company to better serve management for shareholder interests.

After creating the first index fund in the world in 1976, the Vanguard 500, it has since outperformed many other competing large mutual funds. Currently, $100 billion is invested in this mutual fund; since then, many more have been created.

The company is the largest pure no-load mutual fund in the world, known widely for its low-cost index fund. The company also offers actively managed mutual funds and exchange-traded funds, as well as brokerage services, variable and fixed annuities, educational account services, financial planning, asset management, and trust services.

820.714286
mc
m+
m-
mr
c
7
8
9
4
5
6
1
2
3
0
$1,832,550
$10,258,897
8,965,525
169,885

Appendix 2

Case Studies

Case Study: Harry Markowitz

Harry Markowitz is considered one of the fathers of the index fund because his theories throughout his career have defined him as a revolutionary economist.

His Modern Portfolio Theory laid the foundation for many economists who came after him, changing an entire school of thought of how things could be done on the stock market.

For his work, he was awarded the Nobel Prize in Economics in 1990.

How did you become interested in the ideas of David Hume in high school?

On my own time, I read books on philosophy, many of them purchased at used book stores near downtown Chicago. Of these books on philosophy, David Hume's *A Treatise of Human Nature, Book I: Of the Understanding* was the most interesting to me.

What brought you to economics at the University of Chicago?

When I was in high school, I also read science books, especially astronomy and physics, at a popular level, such as the *ABC of Relativity.* When I entered the University of Chicago, I took their two-year bachelor's degree, which consisted of survey courses of various broad fields, such as the physical sciences, social sciences, the humanities, etc. I had learned enough about the physical sciences from my casual reading in high school that Chicago excused me from taking the survey course on the subject. When I finished the two-year bachelor's program and had to choose an upper

Case Study: Harry Markowitz

division, I forgot how much I enjoyed physics and astronomy. I had a recent course in economics as part of the social science survey program. I enjoyed the subject and decided I would become an economist.

Your work in Modern Portfolio Theory is considered the true beginning of the Index Fund Revolution. Can you explain how you came to your realization that the Present Value model by John Burr Williams lacked an understanding of the impact of risk?

When faced with uncertain future dividends, John Burr Williams specified that one should use the mean or expected value of the future dividend stream. If one is only concerned with an expected value of a security, then one must be only interested in the expected value of the portfolio. In order to maximize the expected value of the portfolio, one puts all one's money in the stock with the highest expected return. This was obviously not correct, since investment companies of the day did provide diversification, and everyone knows that one should not "put all of one's eggs in one basket."

How did you come up with the critical line algorithm?

The portfolio selection problem is to minimize variance for various levels of expected return. The critical line algorithm solves this problem. Mostly a small amount of calculus and matrix algebra was the prerequisite for solving the problem at hand.

Did you find it hard to get your portfolio theory accepted, especially as your dissertation?

Not really. Milton Friedman gave me a hard time because he said that the dissertation was not economics, and I wanted a Ph.D. in economics. But I only waited five minutes in the hall for their decision, which was positive; I did get my Ph.D. As for the professional acceptance, I published the results, waited, while nothing happened; Bill Sharpe became interested and involved in the field. Thanks to Bill Sharpe's proselytizing portfolio theory — which I started in the early 1950s — it spread without my help, beginning in the 1960s.

The Markowitz Efficient Portfolio was essential to the creation of the Capital Asset Pricing Model. Can you explain your portfolio theory briefly?

Portfolio theory assumes that the individual investor seeks to find an efficient combination of expected return and variance, i.e., one where you

Case Study: Harry Markowitz

cannot get more expected return without taking on more variance and get less variance without giving up some expected return. Specifically, it assumes that the investor seeks such mean-variance efficiency subject to any system of linear equality or inequality constraints.

Why do you think it took Wall Street and investors so long to accept the idea of index funds? It was 20 years after your theory before the first true index fund appeared, yet the index fund market has seen huge growth in the 1990s and 2000s.

The sequence of ideas was this: I proposed mean-variance efficiency. Bill Sharpe showed that under the assumptions that Capital Asset Pricing Model, a market-wide, capitalization-weighted index fund (plus borrowing or lending perhaps) was the only efficient portfolio. Michael Jensen showed that the money managers of the day were not beating this market portfolio. Wells Fargo decided, "If you can't beat them, join them," and started index funds. In time, index funds and exchange traded funds (ETFs) increased in popularity until they became a large part of capital markets.

How did you find out you won the Nobel Prize?

I was in Japan at the time, teaching at Tokyo University. The Nobel committee did not know how to reach me, so they could not inform me of the Prize. The head of the math department of Tokyo University called me and told me that I had won the Prize and that a reporter from the Tokyo public television station wanted to interview me.

Can you describe what that was like?

Life became very hectic.

What is it like being considered one of the fathers of the Index Fund?

The thought that portfolio theory — with either index funds or individual securities as its basic investments — has become a widely used tool in a trillion dollar industry is more satisfying than even winning of the Nobel Prize.

Case Study: Eugene Fama

Eugene Fama was a forward thinker from the University of Chicago, a breeding ground for revolutionary economists. His Random Walk Theory, which was published in his thesis "The Behavior of Stock Market Prices," was an important development in the creation of the index fund.

Your thesis, "The Behavior of Stock Market Price," deals with the Random Walk Theory, which proved instrumental in the concept of the index fund. What drew you to writing a thesis on that subject matter?

With the advent of computers in the early 1960s, stock market research was a natural, and there was lots of interest among the faculty at Chicago.

What brought you to this hypothesis of the efficient market hypothesis?

My thesis research.

Do you consider yourself a father of the index fund due to your work that led to its creation?

Passive investing in general is a natural result of efficient markets research. I don't know about the father business. Who's the mother?

Appendix 3

Internet Resources

American Association of Individual Investors	http://www.aaii.com
American Stock Exchange	http://amex.com
Austin Coins	http://www.austincoins.com
Bank of England	http://www.bankofengland.co.uk
Barron's	http://www.barronsmag.com
BMA	http://www.bondmarkets.com
Boston Stock Exchange	http://www.bostonstock.com
Briefing.com	http://www.briefing.com
British Banking Association	http://www.bba.org.uk
Bureau of Economic Analysis	http://www.bea.gov
Bureau of Labor Statistics	http://stats.bls.gov

BusinessWeek	http://www.businessweek.com
Census Bureau	http://www.census.gov
Chicago Board of Trade	http://www.cbot.com
Chicago Board Options Exchange	http://www.cboe.com
Chicago Mercantile Exchange	http://www.cme.com
Chicago Stock Exchange	http://www.chx.com
Commodity Futures Trading Commission	http://www.cftc.gov
Cornell University	http://www.law.cornell.edu
Council of Economic Advisors	http://www.whitehouse.gov/cea/
Council of Institutional Investors	http://www.cii.org/about/
Daily Reckoning	http://www.dailyreckoning.com
Deutsche Bundesbank	http://www.bundesbank.de
Dictionary.com	http://www.dictionary.com
Dow Jones Company	http://dowjones.com
Dun & Bradstreet	http://www.dnb.com
Energy Information Agency	http://www.eia.doe.gov
Eurexchange	http://www.eurexchange.com
Euroclear	http://www.euroclear.com
Euronext	http://www.euronext.com
Export-Import Bank of the United States	http://www.exim.gov/

Facts on File	http://www.factsonfile.com
Fannie Mae	http://www.fanniemae.com
Federal Reserve	http://www.federalreserve.gov
Federal Trade Commission	http://ftc.gov
Find Law	http://library.findlaw.com
Fitch Investments	http://www.fitchinv.com
Freddie Mac	http://www.freddiemac.com
G10	http://g10.org/
G24	http://www.g24.org/
Ginnie Mae	http://www.ginniemae.gov/
GrowCo.com	http://www.growco.com
Hyperhistory.com	http://www.hyperhistory.com
Institute for Supply Management	http://www.ism.ws/
International Monetary Fund	http://www.imf.org
International Standards Organization	http://www.iso.org
Investionary.com	http://www.investionary.com
Investors.com	http://www.investors.com
Investorwords.com	http://www.investorwords.com
Kansas City Board of Trade	http://www.kcbt.com
Library of Congress	http://thomas.loc.gov/cgi-bin/bdquery/z?d098:HR00559:

London Metal Exchange	http://www.lme.co.uk
London Online	http://www.londononline.co.uk
MaxPain	http://65.108.12.28/cgi-bin/maxpain.cgi
Moody's Investors Service	http://moodys.com
Morningstar.com	http://morningstar.com/
Municipal Securities Rulemaking Board	http://www.msrb.org/msrb1/
NASD	http://www.nasd.com
NASDAQ	https://www.nasdaq.com
National Association of Investors Corporation	http://www.betterinvesting.org
National Cooperative Bank	http://www.ncb.coop/
National Futures Association	http://www.nfa.futures.org
National Stock Exchange	http://www.nsx.com
New York Board of Trade	http://www.nybot.com/
New York Stock Exchange	http://www.nyse.com
New York University	http://www.nyu.edu
North American Securities Administrators Association	http://www.nasaa.org
NYMEX	http://www.nymex.com
Office of Thrift Supervision	http://www.ots.treas.gov
Opra Data	http://www.opradata.com
PBGC	http://www.pbgc.gov/

Philadelphia Stock Exchange	http://www.phlx.com/
Pink Sheets	http://www.pinksheets.com
Princeton University	http://www.wws.princeton.edu
Public Broadcasting Service	http://www.pbs.org
Public Company Accounting Oversight Board	http://www.pcaobus.org/
Public Investors Arbitration Bar Association	http://www.piaba.org
Reuters	http://www.reuters.com
Securities & Exchange Commission	http://www.sec.gov
Securities Industry Association	http://www.sia.com
Securities Industry Automation Industry	http://siac.com
SIPC	http://www.sipc.org/
Standard & Poor's	http://www.standardandpoors.com
Stock Charts.com	http://stockcharts.com
Teach me Finance.com	http://teachmefinance.com
The Black Vault	http://www.blackvault.com
The Bond Buyer	http://www.bondbuyer.com
Toronto Post	http://www.torontopost.biz
Trading-glossary.com	http://www.trading-glossary.com

Treasury Department	http://www.publicdebt.treas.gov
TSX	http://www.tsx.com
U.S. Bankruptcy Court	http://www.uscourts.gov/
U.S. Department of Justice	http://www.usdoj.gov
U.S. Department of State	http://www.state.gov
U.S. History.com	http://www.u-s-history.com/
U.S. House of Representatives	http://uscode.house.gov/
U.S. Treasury Products	http://www.treasurydirect.gov
U.S. Trademarks Office	http://www.uspto.gov
University of British Columbia	http://fx.sauder.ubc.ca/ECU.html
University of California	http://www.law.uc.edu
University of Pennsylvania	http://www.law.upenn.edu
University of Toronto	http://www.g7.utoronto.ca
USA Today	http://www.usatoday.com
Value Line	http://valueline.com
Value Line	http://www.valueline.com/
Wall Street Journal Classroom	http://wsjclassroom.com
Washington Post	http://www.washingtonpost.com
Wikipedia	http://en.wikipedia.org
World Federation of Exchanges	http://www.world-exchanges.org/
Yahoo Finance	http://finance.yahoo.com

Appendix 4

Acronyms

A/D	Advance/Decline Ratio
AAII	American Association of Individual Investors
ABS	Automated Bond System
ACE	American Stock Exchange
ACH	Automated Clearing House
ADR	American Depositary Receipt
ADS	American Depositary Share
AMBAC	American Municipal Bond Assurance Corporation
AMEX	American Stock Exchange
AON	All or None
APB	Accounting Principles Board
ASAM	Automated Search and Match
AUD	Australian Dollar
BBA	British Banking Association

BDK	Display Book
BEA	Bureau of Economic Analysis
BEX	Boston Equity Exchange
BIF	Bank Insurance Fund
BMA	Bond Market Association
BOD	Board of Directors
BOX	Boston Option Exchange
BOP	Balance of Payments
BSE	Boston Stock Exchange
CAPEX	Capital Expense or Capital Expenditure
CBO	Collateralized Bond Obligation
CBOE	Chicago Board Options Exchange
CBOT	Chicago Board of trade
CD	Certificate of Deposit
CDSL	Contingent Deferred Sales Loan
CEA	Council of Economic Advisers
CEO	Cash Flow
CFAT	Cash Flow after Taxes
CFE	CBOE Futures Exchange

CFO	Chief Financial Officer
CFPS	Cash Flow Per Share
CFRI	Cash Flow Return on Investments
CFTC	Commodity Futures Trading Commission
CH	Swiss Franc
CHX	Chicago Stock Exchange
CND	Canadian Dollar
CNY	Chinese Yuan
COGS	Cost of Goods Sold
COMEX	Commodities Exchange Inc.
COO	Chief Operating Officer
COT	Commitment of Traders Report
CPA	Certified Public Accountant
CPI	Consumer Price Index
CPS	Current Population Survey
CQS	Consolidated Quote System
CRD	Central Registration Depositary
CSCE	Coffee, Sugar, and Cocoa Exchange
CTA	Consolidated Tape Association

CTP	Consolidated Tape Plan
CTS	Consolidated Tape System
CUSIP	Committee on Uniform security Identification Procedures
DAT	Direct Access Trading
DCF	Discounted Cash Flow
DD	Due Diligence
DJIA	Dow Jones Industrial Average
DNR	Do Not Reduce
DPO	Direct Public Offering
DTD	Day to Day
ECN	Electronic Communication Network
ECN	Electronic Communication Network
ECU	European Currency Unit
EDGAR	Electronic Data Gathering Analysis and Retrieval
EMA	Exponential Moving Average
LIFFE	London International Financial Futures and Options Exchange
LIT	Limit if Touched

LOC	Limit on Close
LOO	Limit on Open
LSE	London Stock Exchange
MA	Moving Average
MACD	Moving Average Convergence/Divergence
MBS	Mortgage-Backed Security
MID	Market Index Deposit
MIG	Moody's Investment Grade
MIT	Market if Touched
MRQ	Most Recent Quarter
MSRB	Municipal Securities Rulemaking Board
Mx	Montreal Stock Exchange
NAIC	National Association of Investors Corporation
NASAA	North American Securities Administrators Association
NASD	National Association of Securities Dealers
NBBO	National Best Bid and Offer
NEV	Net Asset Value
NEVPS	Net Asset Value Per Share

NFA	National Futures Association
NIC	Net Interest Cost
NMS	National Market System
NSTS	National Securities Trading System
NSX	Cincinnati Stock Exchange
NYBOT	New York Board of Trade
NYCE	New York Cotton Exchange
NYMEX	New York Mercantile Exchange
NYSE	New York Stock Exchange
OARS	Opening Automated Reporting System
OCIE	Office of Compliance Inspections and Examination
OID	Original Issue Discount
OPRA	Options Price Reporting Authority
OTC	Over-the-counter Market
OTCBB	Over-the-counter Bulletin Board
P&L	Profit and Loss Statement
P/B	Price to Book Ratio
PCAOB	Public Company Accounting Oversight Board

PBGC	Pension Benefit Guaranty Corporation
PCE	Personal Consumption Expenditures
PCX	Pacific Stock Exchange
PE	Price to Earnings Ratio
PERS	Post Execution Reporting System
PHLX	Philadelphia Stock Exchange
PIABA	Public Investors Arbitration Bar Association
PPI	Producer Price Index
REIT	Real Estate Investment Trust
ROA	Rights of Accumulation
ROE	Return on Equity
ROI	Return on Investment
RSI	Relative Strength Index
S&P	Standard & Poor's
SAIF	Savings Association Insurance Fund
SEC	Securities & Exchange Commission
SG&A	Sales, General & Administration
SIPC	Securities Investor Protection Corporation
SOES	Small Order Execution System

SOX	Sarbanes-Oxley Act of 2002
SPDR	Standard & Poor's Depositary Receipt
SRL	Speed Resistance Line
SRO	Self-Regulatory Organization
SSF	Single Stock Futures
STA	Securities Traders Association (STA)
SWX	Swiss Exchange
TRIN	Trading Index
TSE	Toronto Stock Exchange
TSX	Toronto Stock Exchange
TTM	Trailing 12 Months
UCC	Uniform Commercial Code
UIT	Unit Investment Trust
UPC	Uniform Practice Code
USD	U.S. Dollar
YOY	Year-over-year

Appendix 5

Investor Resources: Getting Help When You Need It

INVESTMENT ADVISER REGISTRATION DEPOSITORY: A NASD-developed and operated system that maintains registration and disclosure information on registered investment advisors, located at **www.iard.com**.

ADVISORY NEWSLETTER A publication that provides market commentary and investment recommendations. Most advisory newsletters are subscriptions services. See Hulbert Financial Digest.

AMERICAN ASSOCIATION OF INDIVIDUAL INVESTORS (AAII) A networking and education organization for individual investors. On the Web at **www.aaii.com**.

BARRON'S A weekly finance magazine published by Dow Jones, Inc. It is available in print format or an online subscription. It is available online at **www.barrons.com**.

BOND BUYER, THE A daily publication for the bond market that contains a comprehensive listing of municipal bond data. The Bond Buyer was established in 1891 and is also known as The Daily Bond Buyer. On the Web at **www.bondbuyer.com**.

BOND MARKET ASSOCIATION (BMA) A trade association comprised of banks, dealers, brokers, and underwriters of debt instruments. The BMA also provides educational services to individual investors. On the Web at **www.bondmarkets.com**.

CERTIFIED FUND SPECIALIST A financial professional who possesses a certificate attesting to his or her qualification to advise clients on the selection of mutual fund investments.

COMMODITY TRADING ADVISOR A person who is registered with the Commodity Futures Trading Commission (CFTC) to provide, advise, and manage futures and options trading activity for another person.

COMPUSTAT A subscription service from Standard & Poor's that provides market information and fundamental data.

DUN & BRADSTREET (D&B) A business and finance research company that issues corporate credit ratings and maintains a database of financial information on corporations worldwide. A company's D&B rating can affect both its stock price and its bond rating. On the Web at **www.dnb.com**.

EDGAR ONLINE A publicly traded company that provides value added data services based on the Securities & Exchange Commission's EDGAR database of corporate filings. EDGAR Online trades under the symbol EDGR on NASDAQ and is online at **www.edgar-online.com**.

FEDERAL REGISTER A government publication that provides public notice of new regulations from the Office of Thrift Supervision, legal notices, presidential proclamations, executive orders, documents required by an Act of Congress, and other official documents of public interest. The Federal Register is published daily, Monday through Friday and is available on the Web at **www.gpoaccess.gov/fr/index.html**.

FITCH INVESTORS SERVICE The company that issues the Fitch Ratings for the bond, Eurobond, and funds market. Compare to Moody's Investors Service and Standard & Poor's. See Bond Ratings.

HULBERT FINANCIAL DIGEST A MarketWatch/Dow Jones subscription service that rates advisory newsletters by tracking and measuring their recommendations against actual performance. The digest is available by e-mail or U.S. Postal Service delivery. On the Web at **www.marketwatch.com**.

INVESTMENT ADVISER REGISTRATION DEPOSITORY A NASD-developed and operated system that maintains registration and disclosure information on registered investment advisors. On the Web at **www.iard.com**.

INVESTMENT ADVISOR A professional hired by an individual to provide financial and investment advice. See Registered Investment Advisor (RIA); Trailer Fee.

INVESTOR PROTECTION TRUST A non-profit organization that provides resources to help individual investors make informed investment decisions. On the Web at **www.investorprotection.org**.

INVESTORS BUSINESS DAILY (IBD) A daily financial newspaper and Internet-based investment news and information resource. On the Web at **www.investors.com**.

MOODY'S INVESTORS SERVICE A financial research firm opining on the creditworthiness of bond issuers. See Bond Rating. On the Web at **www.moodys.com**.

MORNINGSTAR, INC. An investment research and rating service for mutual funds, stocks, closed-end funds, Exchange Traded Funds, hedge funds, and other investments. On the Web at **www.morningstar.com**.

NATIONAL ASSOCIATION OF INVESTORS CORPORATION (NAIC) A networking and education organization for individual investors.

REUTERS A global business and financial news service. In addition to news content for media organizations, Reuters provides financial information products to businesses, financial professionals, and investors. One the Web at **www.reuters.com**.

STANDARD & POOR'S A market research firm that publishes credit ratings and financial reports used by individuals and institutional investors. It is also the originator of the family of S&P indexes, the best known and most closely watched of which is the S&P 500. On the Web at **www.standardandpoors.com**.

VALUE LINE, INC. An investment research firm with product offerings for individual, professional, and institutional investors. Value Line is known for the Value Line Investment Survey for stock analysis, but the company has similar products for mutual funds and options as well. On the Web at **www.valueline.com**.

WALL STREET JOURNAL, THE A financial news publication from Dow Jones & Company. It is available in print daily and online. The weekly and Sunday editions are delivered each Saturday morning and Sunday mornings, respectively. On the Web at **www.wsj.com**.

Bibliography

Hebner, Mark T. (2005) *Index Funds: The 12-step Program For Active Investors*. IFA Publishing.

Schoenfeld, Steven A. (2004) *Active Index Investing.* Hoboken, New Jersey. John Wiley and Sons Inc.

Ferri, Richard A. (2007) *All About Index Funds,* Second Edition. New York, New York. McGraw-Hill Companies Inc.

Swedroe, Larry E. (2001) *What Wall Street Doesn't Want You To Know*. New York, New York. St. Martin's Press.

Author Biography

Craig Baird is a professional writer from British Columbia who spends his time writing books and hiking the mountains around his home. Prior to being a writer, he was a computer network administrator looking for a change. Today, he spends his days writing books for himself and his clients from all over the world. He has also written Atlantic Publishing's *The Six Sigma Manual for Small and Medium Businesses: What You Need to Know, Explained Simply.*

DAILY COMPOSITE
TRACKING THE FTSE BURSA SECOND BOARD
DAILY TOP 10 ACTIVE STOCKS
December 13
6,000.93
1,423.72
DOWN

Glossary

Application: The application is a form that comes with a fund's prospectus. Investors open accounts with mutual funds by completing the application, which asks for basic information from the investor, including name, type of account, tax identification number, and service option choices. When completed, the application, along with a check made payable to the fund, is mailed to the fund company.

Assets: As an accounting or investment term, assets refer to owned items, such as cash, stock, equipment, and real estate.

Bond: A bond is a contract representing the terms of borrowing and repayment for a debt. Also see *Security*.

Broker: A broker, also called a Registered Representative or account executive, is a licensed person authorized to receive commissions. Brokers are always affiliated with a brokerage company or broker-dealer. The broker-dealer is responsible for oversight of their affiliated brokers. Brokers normally work for commissions, while Registered Investment Advisors work for fees.

Distribution: A distribution is a dividend payable to investors. A dividend can be of three types: income, short-term capital gain, or long-term capital gain. While we are on the subject, be aware that a mutual fund dividend or distribution may be physically paid to the investor, or it may be reinvested in the fund, giving the investor more shares.

Diversification: Diversification refers to the numbers of securities held and their types. For example, ten stocks would constitute a more diversified portfolio than two stocks. In addition, the concept of diversification extends beyond the confines of a single type of investment. For example, there is more diversification in a stock and bond portfolio than in a portfolio constructed entirely of stocks alone.

Dividends: Dividends are payments made by corporations on earnings. In other words, part of the profits and income are shared with investors. This applies not only to mutual funds, but to shares of companies as well. Dividends from mutual funds may be of three types: income dividends, short-term capital gains dividends, and long-term capital gains.

Economies of Scale: Economies of scale refers to the savings that companies may experience when they grow. For example, it may be cheaper, on a per-employee basis, to produce payroll for ten employees than for one because it is being done regardless.

Growth: Growth refers to capital appreciation. The underlying value of the investment is expected to grow. Unlike income, which is regular and consistent in most cases, growth is much less certain. Growth investments more often than not outpace the returns on income-type investments over five to ten years or longer.

Income: Income refers to the generation of regular earnings, whether from interest on bonds or from corporate dividends. Growth and income are somewhat mutually exclusive. For example, a fast-growing technology company may choose to reinvest earnings for further rapid growth, leaving little cash for dividend distributions to shareholders.

Index: Indexes are numerical calculations based on groups of similar investments, meant to convey the overall price level of a given market. For example, there are indexes for blue chip stocks, small stocks, foreign stocks, Treasury Bonds, and so on. Examples of indexes you may have heard of are the Dow Jones 30 Industrials, the Standard and Poor's 500 Index, the Russell 2000 index, and the MSCI EAFE (Europe, Australia, Far East) index.

Industry: Mutual funds usually are well-diversified. A stock fund, for example, normally will be invested not only in a wide variety of individual stocks, but also a variety of industries, such as utilities, technology, consumer durable goods, health care, retail, and so on. Funds that focus on particular industries lack a degree of diversification and thus are subject to increased risk.

Investment Company: Investment company is another term for mutual fund. It is a company designed for investment and is organized as a corporation, distributing shares and paying dividends.

Issue: A security made available to the public may be called an issue. On this basis, mutual funds issue shares to investors in return for cash.

Liability: What a person or company owes to others. The opposite of an asset.

Load: Another word for sales charge. A load is added to the net asset value of many mutual funds to come up with a public selling price. For example, if a fund's shares are worth $10 and the load is 5 percent, then the offering price to the public would be $10.50 ($10 plus 5 percent, or $.50). The load, or sales charge, is paid to the selling brokerage firm, which in turn pays out much of it to the individual broker as a commission. Thus, in our example above, only $10 actually goes into the fund; the other $.50 goes to the brokerage firm.

Management: Management, or manager, is a broad term that, in the mutual fund world, refers to the people who select the actual investments of a mutual fund.

Marking-to-Market: A process (required of mutual funds, by law) of adjusting the price of shares to a current market value, based on the value of the underlying holdings.

Money Market: Money market has come to mean a certain type of bank account as a result of heavy marketing by bankers. Yet the term actually refers to debt instruments (bonds) that mature within one year. A money market mutual fund invests in money market instruments. Bonds maturing at dates better than one year out are part of the capital market. In both cases, the terms refer to the uses to which the proceeds of the bond issues are used: as money (liquid) or for capital investment (machinery, longer-term investments).

Morningstar: Morningstar, Inc. is an investment research and information company based in Chicago, Illinois. Morningstar pioneered in-depth, timely mutual fund information service called Morningstar Mutual Funds, which has become the standard in mutual fund research.

Mutual Fund: A broad term meaning an investment company or trust that is owned by investors and is subject to regulations as described in the Investment Company Act of 1940.

Net Assets: When you add up the value of assets, and deduct liabilities, you arrive at the net value of assets over liabilities, or net assets.

Net Asset Value: In mutual fund parlance, this is the value per share. It is arrived at by taking the company's net assets and dividing by the number of shares outstanding.

No-Load: A broad term applied to mutual funds that have no sales charges or commissions.

No-Load Fund Analyst: The *No-Load Fund Analyst* is a mutual fund newsletter published by Litman/Gregory in the San Francisco Bay Area. This newsletter has some unique strengths, including regular in-depth interviews with top fund managers, their backgrounds, and their techniques and investment philosophy. In addition to fund reviews, the *No-Load Fund Analyst* discusses economic trends and the relative values of various asset classes at different points in time.

Objective: The objective of a mutual fund briefly tells what the chief goal of the fund is, often in 25 words or fewer. For example, a fund's primary investment may be "growth with income as a secondary consideration," or "the highest level of income consistent with preservation of capital." As in food labels, the first items mentioned are frequently the most important!

Offering Price: The offering price is the price an investor pays per share of a mutual fund. It is the total cost per share and may include a sales charge.

Open-End Mutual Fund: A type of mutual fund that is designed to issue and redeem shares from investors directly, rather than through the secondary (stock) market.

Portfolio: A term denoting the overall collection of securities or investments owned by a person or company.

Prospectus: The prospectus is a mutual fund's offering memorandum. It is a small booklet, on average about 30 pages long, that gives basic information designed to disclose relevant facts that investors need to make an informed decision about investing in a given fund. Federal regulations require prospectuses to cover certain basic important information, such as the fund's investment objective, expenses, management agreements, risks, and how to do business with the fund.

Sales Charge: A commission or extra cost added on top of the price of a mutual fund when you buy it. The amount is calculated as a percentage of the underlying value per share. The sales charge is paid to a brokerage company and is not invested in the fund. In other words, it is simply a cost to the investor off the top, lost to the investor at the start.

Sector: Sector is another word for industry. Sector funds frequently focus on a single industry, such as health care, technology, or utilities. These funds are best avoided until investors gain a fair amount of investment expertise at a minimum. In any event, investors should endeavor to build a properly diversified portfolio before venturing into these specialty funds.

Security: A document representing participation in an investment. Stocks are securities representing ownership shares. Bonds are securities representing a contractual debt obligation of the issuer to repay the holder with interest.

Shares: Shares are units of ownership in a corporation. For shares in a mutual fund, the ownership value of each share may be determined by dividing the net assets by the number of shares. The value of shares in a publicly-traded stock is determined by supply-and-demand only, and may or may not bear any discernible correlation with the value of the company's assets.

Shareholder: A mutual fund shareholder is an investor in a fund. He or she owns shares in the fund as a result of the investment being made. Normally, shares may be purchased or redeemed for cash at any time.

Statements: Statements are periodic reports to investors regarding their investment accounts. Statements regularly contain the name and address of the account holder, date of the statement, current number of shares, current value per share, recent transactions that have occurred, such as purchases and dividends, and the total account value. Year-end mutual fund summaries, showing all transactions for the preceding year, should be kept by investors as long as the account is open for tax calculation purposes, and then for a period of at least three years.

Stock: A type of investment security, denominated in shares that represent ownership in a company.

Trading: Trading refers to the buying and selling of investments, such as stocks and bonds, for a mutual fund.

Index

E

F

G

H

I

J

L

M

N

O

P

R

S